Doing Essays & Assignments

SAGE was founded in 1965 by Sara Miller McCune to support the dissemination of usable knowledge by publishing innovative and high-quality research and teaching content. Today, we publish over 900 journals, including those of more than 400 learned societies, more than 800 new books per year, and a growing range of library products including archives, data, case studies, reports, and video. SAGE remains majority-owned by our founder, and after Sara's lifetime will become owned by a charitable trust that secures our continued independence.

Los Angeles | London | New Delhi | Singapore | Washington DC | Melbourne

2nd Edition

Pete Greasley

Doing
Essays
& Assignments

Essential Tips for Students

Los Angeles | London | New Delhi
Singapore | Washington DC | Melbourne

Los Angeles | London | New Delhi
Singapore | Washington DC | Melbourne

SAGE Publications Ltd
1 Oliver's Yard
55 City Road
London EC1Y 1SP

SAGE Publications Inc.
2455 Teller Road
Thousand Oaks, California 91320

SAGE Publications India Pvt Ltd
B 1/I 1 Mohan Cooperative Industrial Area
Mathura Road
New Delhi 110 044

SAGE Publications Asia-Pacific Pte Ltd
3 Church Street
#10-04 Samsung Hub
Singapore 049483

Editor: Jai Seaman
Editorial assistant: Aly Owen
Production editor: Tom Bedford
Copyeditor: Richard Leigh
Proofreader: Sarah Cooke
Marketing manager: Catherine Slinn
Cover design: Shaun Mercier
Typeset by: C&M Digitals (P) Ltd, Chennai, India
Printed in India at Replika Press Pvt Ltd

First edition published 2011
This second edition published 2016

Library of Congress Control Number: 2015959031

British Library Cataloguing in Publication data

A catalogue record for this book is available from
the British Library

ISBN 978-1-4739-1206-9
ISBN 978-1-4739-1207-6 (pbk)

At SAGE we take sustainability seriously. Most of our products are printed in the UK using FSC papers and boards.
When we print overseas we ensure sustainable papers are used as measured by the PREPS grading system.
We undertake an annual audit to monitor our sustainability.

Contents

List of figures

List of tables

About the author

Pete Greasley has been marking student assignments for more years than he would care to remember, and not particularly enjoying it. He has conducted research and published academic articles in psychology, sociology, health, and education, and has also written an introductory book on quantitative data analysis. Research and teaching interests include psychological and social issues relating to health, sceptical inquiry relating to pseudo-science and the paranormal, and how to help students avoid common mistakes when writing their assignments. He currently spends much of his time supervising trainee clinical psychologists doing their research projects at Lancaster University.

Preface to the second edition

When SAGE contacted me to produce a second edition of this book I was initially quite flattered. I was also quite excited because it would give me the opportunity to make some changes and improve the book. That was initially. Then I remembered what my life was like when I was writing the book, which I had so enthusiastically embarked upon, but then three years down the line so eagerly boxed up and shoved in the attic; done, finished, and never again. Returning to the book would be like opening up an old wound: back to working evenings and weekends and, worst of all, more arguments with Wendy as she tells me I can't write and crosses everything out unceremoniously, and somewhat condescendingly. But despite all this, and purely for the benefit 'my students' I returned once more, unto the fray.

This new edition contains three new chapters providing tips relating to common assignments: presentations, group projects, and literature reviews. There are also many other additions and changes throughout the original chapters. And I've added a few cartoons.

Acknowledgements

First of all I'd like to thank all the students whose assignments I've had the pleasure to mark, particularly those which were virtually unreadable, poorly structured, mainly descriptive, partly plagiarised, and generally lost sight of the question; without you this book would not have been written. Second, thanks to Elizabeth Blythe for submitting one of the best assignments I've read and allowing me to include it as an example assignment. Third, thanks to all those tutors who took the time to respond to the survey upon which this book is based (these are not just my tips – they're yours). Fourth, thanks to my colleague Andrea Cassidy for her moral support and collaboration on the survey. Fifth, thanks to all those at SAGE who helped to produce the book, particularly Patrick Brindle for his mentorship in the early stages and, latterly, to David Hodge, Ian Antcliff and Sarah Bury for their advice (and forbearance) on the home stretch. And finally, deepest gratitude to Wendy Calvert for her indefatigable editing and proofreading, for striking out swathes of so-called 'irrelevant text', and for pointing out that my section on being clear and concise wasn't clear and concise.

I'd also like to acknowledge *Times Higher Education* for allowing me to include the speech to new undergraduates by the Head of Student Satisfaction at Poppleton University.

For this second edition I would also like to thank the people from SAGE who were involved in producing the book: Jai Seaman, Lilly Mehrbod, Alysha Owen, Tom Bedford, and the very thorough copyeditor, Richard Leigh.

Why you should read this book (and keep it to yourself)

I started writing these tips when I realised that many students were making the same common mistakes in their assignments. It was happening year after year – different students, same mistakes. So it occurred to me that I had two options:

Option 1 Produce a list of the most frequent comments so that I could simply copy and paste them into the mark sheets, e.g. 'Not enough detail', 'Too much detail', 'Which question were you answering?', 'What's this reference to essaysrus.com?'

Or

Option 2 Provide some guidance for students highlighting these common problems in the hope that if they are listed somewhere then they might be avoided in the future.

Well, the second option prevailed and here it is.

The result is a fairly comprehensive list of tips and techniques to help students avoid common mistakes and adopt strategies to improve their assignments. So, if you've been stunned by a mark of 26% when you were used to getting straight As at college last year, or if you're one of those students who complains 'I always get a mark in the 50s whatever I do', this book should help you to see where you're going wrong. Equally, if you're particularly ambitious to achieve the highest grades, but can't seem to make the jump from a second to a first, these tips should provide you with an insight into what's required to raise your game.

Winston Churchill (1874–1965) has been quoted as saying that 'Success is the ability to go from one failure to another with no loss of enthusiasm'. It's also the ability to learn from your mistakes and get some good advice from people who know what they're talking about. In this respect, it's important to point out that the tips in this book are not just my tips – they are based on a survey of 32 university tutors who were asked to list the things that frustrate and impress them when marking assignments. This is a relatively small sample, but think of it this way: if each of these tutors had, on average, 10 years' experience of marking, then you're reaping the benefit from 320 years of student assessment.

So you'll be gaining a valuable insight into the minds of the tutors who mark your assignments – what they like and what they dislike – as well as some practical advice on what you need to do if you want to get high marks. This is why you need to keep the tips in this book to yourself: if all the students on your course follow these tips, it will raise the standard of all assignments – and yours won't stand out as much! Here's a brief outline of what's covered in each of the chapters.

Chapter 1: An insight into the marking process

In this chapter you'll gain an insight into the marking process, which will help you to see things from the tutor's perspective. They will usually have lots of assignments to mark and not much time in which to mark them. This being the case, it's important to help your poor tutor through this ordeal by making sure that your assignment is a 'smooth ride' rather than a 'bone-shaker'. We'll also look at different approaches to learning (are you an 'explorer' or a 'tourist'?), consistency (and inconsistency) across markers, different types of marker (is your tutor a 'hawk' or a 'dove'?), and potential sources of bias that may influence the grade awarded (including what you look like).

Chapter 2: How to impress and how to distress markers

If you're interested in knowing what tutors look for when they mark assignments – what impresses them and what frustrates them – then this chapter provides some answers. It presents the results from a survey of tutors who were asked to address these two questions by listing common problems in student assignments and strategies that impress them. So you'll gain an insight into what tutors are really looking for when they mark assignments – what they like, what they dislike, what impresses them, and what annoys them. You'll also see what the most common mistakes are in assignments (so you can avoid them in your own) and what has the most positive impact on the mark.

Chapter 3: Before you start, some rules of the game

Are there certain 'rules of the game' at universities when it comes to writing assignments and achieving higher grades? This chapter reveals the strategies used by successful students to gain top marks, in particular, adopting the role of the 'cue-seeker' and taking a deep/strategic approach to learning. The chapter also looks at some of the more dubious tactics that have been used by students to gain higher marks, and concludes with a survey of cheating behaviours.

Chapter 4: Getting started ... and getting finished

This chapter provides some strategies to help you get started with your assignment and keep it focused by having the conclusion in mind from the beginning. A range of tools and techniques for planning the assignment and time management are discussed (mind maps, weekly timetables, Gantt charts), as well as guidance on the amount of time it should take to write an assignment, along with the stages involved.

Chapter 5: Reading and researching the literature

In this chapter we'll be looking at the types of references you should be citing – and not citing – in your assignments (bearing in mind that one university department voted to ban references to Wikipedia). We'll also see the importance of taking into account different perspectives when reviewing the literature, along with the need to use reliable (rather than 'dodgy') sources of information. The message being that, just because something has been published in a book or an academic journal, this does not mean it is 'the truth'.

Chapter 6: Introductions, conclusions and structure

A good introduction and a good conclusion are crucial for a first-class assignment. This chapter provides some useful advice on how to write an introduction using five key criteria that could, according to one research study, increase the grade of your assignment. There's also advice about writing conclusions (three key criteria) and how to structure your assignment using signposting and headings. And if you're aware of the 'halo effect', you'll know why the introduction to your assignment may be especially important.

Chapter 7: What was the question again?

Failing to answer the question and address the assignment guidelines is a common problem amongst students. In this chapter we'll discuss the importance of analysing the assignment question, defining key terms, and reminding the tutor how the information you are discussing in your assignment is addressing the question (avoiding the 'so what?' comment). The importance of consulting and addressing the marking criteria for an assignment is also discussed, along with the need to make the transition from 'unconscious incompetence' to 'unconscious competence'.

Chapter 8: Critical analysis, perspective and argument

If you're looking for the really high marks, your assignment will need to include some critical analysis, perspective and argument, especially as you progress through the years at university. In this chapter we'll examine the six levels of thinking you'll need to rise through if you're seeking the highest marks, along with the need to adopt a position, construct an argument, and make a case for the position you have adopted. We'll also see that there are no 'right' answers, and that you should trust no one.

Chapter 9: The greatest source of 'marker distress': language, grammar and expression

Problems with language, grammar and expression are one of the most common sources of 'marker distress', and may have a considerable impact on the mark if you fail to communicate your ideas clearly. This chapter provides guidance on how to be clear and concise, along with advice about using quotations and acronyms, how to paraphrase what others have written, which 'voice' to write in (first person, third person or the impersonal voice), and how to avoid being nominated for the Bad Writing contest.

Chapter 10: Referencing - an academic fetish for the anally retentive?

In this chapter we'll see why that thing you do at the end of your assignment in a slapdash rush, known as referencing, may be more important than you think when it comes to awarding marks. The chapter includes a quick guide to referencing for the most common sources of information (books, journals, websites) and a 'spot the problems' referencing quiz using award-winning articles from the Ig Nobel prize.

Chapter 11: Plagiarism

This chapter is for you if you have a 'poorly developed authorial identity', for example, copying and pasting large chunks of text that someone else has written and pretending you've written it yourself. It's usually referred to as 'plagiarism'. In this chapter we'll look at different ways to commit plagiarism (including plagiarising yourself), the means by which tutors are able to detect it (e.g. using plagiarism detection software), and how to get the cheapest deal if you're paying an essay writing company to write your assignment. And we'll look at the consequences if you're caught.

Chapter 12: How not to present graphs and charts

When graphs and charts feature in an assignment they are a potential source of marker distress and amusement. This chapter provides some tips on how not to present information in graphs (using examples from student assignments), along with some advice about how to mislead with statistics.

Chapter 13: Presenting your assignment: first impressions count

First impressions are important, so this chapter focuses on how your assignment looks to the tutor when s/he takes it from the pile, glances at the first page and flicks through it. There's advice about 'white space' and avoiding challenging binders, and why you should never, ever, put each page of your assignment in a separate plastic envelope. It also helps if you can spell the tutor's name correctly on the assignment submission sheet and remember the correct name of the module you are studying.

Chapter 14: Feedback and feed-forward

Feedback is crucial for learning, and in this chapter we'll see that there are two kinds of feedback: 'summative' and 'formative' (one is better than the other). But there's also feed-forward of course. In this respect, the chapter includes a very useful checklist of tips that you might wish to complete prior to submitting your assignment to help ensure that you've done all you can to increase your mark!

Chapter 15: Writing research/project reports

If you need to conduct a research study as part of your degree this chapter provides some essential tips for writing up the report. There is a formal structure for reporting research that should be adhered to because it helps you to document precisely what you did and why you did it. The aim is to write the report with such clarity and preciseness that somebody else could read it and replicate your study by doing exactly what you did.

Chapter 16: Doing a systematic literature review

Many students need to do a literature review as part of their assignments or, indeed, as an assignment in itself. This chapter provides some tips on how to conduct a systematic literature review, including how to choose an appropriate topic, conduct a systematic search of the literature, and report the results of your search clearly and systematically. The importance of systematic literature reviews is discussed and the need to retain a critical perspective on the accuracy of the academic literature is highlighted – especially since, according to one source, 'most published research findings are false'.

Chapter 17: Doing presentations: a fate worse than death?

Are you looking forward to doing presentations as part of your course? No? Didn't think so. This chapter provides a few key tips based on a survey of tutors who were asked, 'What key advice would you give to students about doing presentations?' For the particularly anxious amongst you there's also advice from the realm of psychological therapies on how to allay any tendencies towards 'catastrophic thinking'.

Chapter 18: Group project work, or 'Hell is other people!'

Looking forward to doing group projects as part of your course? That would depend on your attitude to working with other people, and who the other people are. Either way, most projects in the real world require teamwork, so in scheduling group project work your university is providing you with skills for life! This chapter provides tips based on a survey of tutors who were asked, 'What key advice would you give to students about doing group projects?' The second most important thing is to ensure that your project is clearly defined and planned, and there are some useful project management techniques to help with this, but the most important thing is dealing with other people.

1

An insight into the marking process

In this chapter you'll gain an insight into the marking process so you can see how things look from the tutor's perspective. In particular, we'll be looking at:

- The importance of bearing in mind that your tutor will have lots of assignments to mark and limited time to mark them

- The marking process at universities (which may involve up to three stages)

- Consistency across markers, and why some *inconsistency* might actually be a good thing

- Different types of markers ('hawks' and 'doves'), and sources of bias that can influence the mark you're awarded (including what you look like)

- How the transition from school/college to university may be a culture shock for some students

Marking assignments: four in an hour?

Let's start by putting things into context. How many assignments does a typical tutor mark at the end of a typical term? Well, it varies of course, so I decided to take stock of my own marking at the end of a recent term. I compiled a list of:

- all the courses I taught (there were five courses with a total of seven written assignments)

- the number of words for each assignment (most were 2,000 words, but some were 8,000; the average worked out at around 3,000)

- the number of students on each course (200 students in total)

I then multiplied the number of words for each assignment by the number of students and finally summed up the total to reveal a staggering 510,000 (over *half a million*) words. Now, I'm not presenting these statistics for the sympathy vote; rather, the aim is to illustrate where your assignment stands in the grand scheme of things. The point is that, in the midst of this deluge of marking, assignments which are poorly presented and/or difficult to follow may receive relatively short shrift, especially when there is limited time in which to mark them.

This raises another question: How much time do you think a tutor spends marking an assignment? Well, although it may have taken you weeks to prepare and write your 2,000-word assignment (or not, as the case may be), the tutor will probably spend around 30 minutes reading and marking it. This includes writing up the comments. Obviously, this will vary depending on the tutor and the assignment. Some tutors will spend less time on each assignment, believing that 'you should be able to mark four in an hour'. Really. According to one study by Norton (1990), the average time spent marking an assignment of 1,250 words was about 20 minutes; three of the six tutors in the study took less than 15 minutes. Four in an hour.

The marking journey: a 'smooth ride' or a 'bone-shaker'?

So, we've established two things about the marking of assignments: (1) there are lots of them to mark; (2) there is limited time to mark them.

This being the case, what is a tutor looking for in an assignment? Well, perhaps the bare minimum might be termed a 'smooth ride'. What does this mean? It means that I can read your 2,000-word assignment in roughly half an hour without having to stop every few sentences to make comments due to lack of clarity, problems with presentation, incorrect referencing, or generally because I don't have a clue what you're talking about. Think of it as going on a journey: the easier you make it for me to get from A to B the better; a poor assignment is like a journey in which you've made me stop every few minutes – due to traffic jams (unclear language or purpose), red lights (errors) or to check the route (poor structure and presentation). A good assignment gives me a clear run; a very good assignment includes interesting scenery on the way.

The learning journey: are you a hitch-hiker, an explorer, or just plain lost?

Interestingly, a similar analogy is proposed by Walter Skok (2003) and developed by Colin Neville (2009a), in which the grading of assignments is likened to a 'journey of learning' whereby the approach to study adopted by students will be reflected in their grade achieved for assignments. I've summarised the themes in Table 1.1.

Table 1.1 Learning as a journey

Grade	Approach	Characteristics
A	Explorer	Someone who explores the destination thoroughly and independently, venturing beyond the 'given' into new territories and experiences
B	Traveller	Someone who wants to acquire more knowledge of a country – to learn its culture, language, history and current position in the world
C	Tourist	Opts for the package holiday where they are told what to do rather than discover for themselves
D	Hitch-hiker	Someone who may often have to wander off the track (or 'point'), not adopting the most direct and efficient route from A to B
Fail	Lost	Fails to work out clearly where they are going (or why), so becomes lost

The guidelines in this book are primarily designed to make my journey as a marker of assignments easier, but they should hopefully also make you, as a writer of assignments, a more interesting guide.

An insight into the marking process

The marking process will vary across different universities and departments, but in the UK it typically involves three stages:

- **Step 1: First marking**. Usually by your course/module tutor.

- **Step 2: Internal moderation**. 'Moderation' refers to the process for ensuring that marks awarded are fair, consistent and reliable. It's more commonly known as second marking or double-marking by another tutor.

- **Step 3: External moderation**. Where a tutor from another university (an 'external examiner') comments on the marks awarded.

Let's have at look at this process in more detail.

Step 1: First marking

So what happens to your assignment after you've handed it in? Well, once it's been processed by admin:

1. Tutor comes into work to find four piles of assignments on his desk, each over a foot high

2. Tutor takes gun from holster and puts to head (or...)

3. Tutor takes essays home to mark the next day

4. On a nice summer's day, tutor sets up sun-lounger in back garden and settles down to marking (with increasing quantities of 'liquid refreshment')

5. Tutor gets half-way through first assignment and scuttles back indoors due to: electric chainsaw, house alarms, barking dogs, gusty wind blowing pages everywhere …

6. Having read the assignment and made notes, the marking grid is consulted and the marks are entered accordingly, along with copious written feedback helping the student to address the identified areas of deficit. Repeat 100+ times.

The last point about feedback is important. In order to learn and improve you need good feedback: *feedback for learning.* So, if your assignment comes back with a mark of 44% and the only comment you get is 'well done' or 'argument rather thin', you might complain that this is not a great help. What you should be looking for (and asking for) is constructive feedback – comments that will help you to improve future assignments – not only what you haven't done, but, most importantly, what you need to do in future to get a higher mark. In the final chapter we'll be looking at the crucial role of feedback (and feed-forward) in more detail.

In recent years there has been a move towards online submission and marking of assignments. Where this is the case, the tutor will first check the assignment for plagiarism (copying without acknowledging the source, discussed in Chapter 11) to see what percentage of the text matches other sources – from books, websites, journal articles, and student essays (including your own previous submissions). This can be done automatically using a software program called Turnitin, which colour-codes the assignment according to the amount of text that matches other sources – see Figure 1.1. Once the colour turns to red it immediately starts flashing and an alarm alerts the plagiarism police; within minutes there will be a knock on the student's door and they are never seen again.

Well, it's not quite as simple as that, because Turnitin highlights *everything* that matches to other sources, including references and quotes that you have acknowledged with a citation. But, if Turnitin highlights large passages of text that are matched to other sources *without citations*, that's when alarm bells ring (not literally). In a blatant case of plagiarism, the assignment will be subject to

Essay	Colour	% Matching other sources
Student 1	Red	75–100%
Student 2	Orange	50–74%
Student 3	Yellow	25–49%
Student 4	Green	1–24%

Figure 1.1   Online plagiarism reports

investigation. And when all the other students in your class are congratulating or commiserating with each other about their mark, you'll be opening a mysterious letter inviting you to see the tutor for a discussion about your assignment … (the 'P' word may not be mentioned, initially); you may also be summoned to an academic standards committee.

Not that I want to worry you. I recall once having a group of students in my office who were petrified that every little match (words and phrases) between their assignments and others could lead to a charge of plagiarism. Avoiding plagiarism is about writing in your own words and ensuring sources are cited accurately. There's a lot more on this in Chapter 11.

So, assuming that the tutor has checked the assignment for plagiarism, and found it to be acceptable, he will then mark it. The key advantage of marking online is that it saves on paper and admin, and the tutor can create a 'bank' of frequently used comments that can be quickly inserted into the assignment, e.g. 'good argument', 'citation needed', 'unclear expression', 'check spelling', 'wrong', 'very wrong', 'where do I start?', 'ridiculous', 'bizarre', 'I'm losing the will to live here', 'help me'.

From a student's point of view, online submission saves on printing and enables feedback to be provided earlier because there is less administration involved. There can, however, be problems uploading assignments leading to anxious emails and phone calls. If you have a problem submitting your assignment online, my advice is to email it by the deadline, but be aware that this may mean extra work for the tutor if they have to upload the assignment for you (and probably not just you). This is for emergencies only – check with your tutor for their preferences in case of problems like this.

Step 2: Second marking (in moderation)

The process for second marking will vary across departments and universities, but once the first marker (usually your course tutor) has marked the assignments a selection may be passed on to another tutor for 'second marking' (especially when the marks contribute to your final degree classification). Typically, this will be a sample (10–20%) of the assignments representing the range of grades – top, middle, bottom, including 'borderlines' (e.g. 49%, 59%) and all 'fails'.

Second marking may be done independently or 'blindly', that is, where the second marker does not know the grade awarded by the first marker (so they come to an independent decision about the mark), but often 'second marking' is more like a 'second opinion': the second marker does see the grade and the comments from the first marker. Their role, then, is to check the reliability of the marks (are they fair, consistent, too generous or too harsh?) and comment on the feedback provided (does it reflect the mark and promote learning?). Where there is significant disagreement about the mark (e.g. if the second marker thinks it should be in the 60s rather than the 50s), a final mark may be negotiated – keeping in mind that the first marker will usually have the most influence, having taught the course and set the assignment. Sometimes the mark might be averaged, or if there's serious disagreement it might be passed on to another tutor for a third opinion.

Step 3: External moderation

In the UK, a further check is used to help ensure the marking is fair and comparable across universities. 'External examiners' (tutors from other universities) are asked to look at a cross-section of work from all courses and comment on the standard of the assignments and the marks awarded.

Marking assignments: the human factor

Now as we all know, if you ask two different tutors to mark the same assignment you will get two different marks, but hopefully they won't differ too much. Marking assignments, particularly essays in the arts, humanities and social sciences, is not an objective science: it's a judgement, not a measure. All tutors will have their own particular values about what's important in an assignment, which is why specific marking criteria can help to make the process less subjective (there's an outline of some typical marking criteria in Chapter 7, Tip 41). But the idea of arriving at a particular percentage point for a 2,000-word essay will always be an approximation (which is why many tutors find the idea of marking in broader grades or marking bands preferable).

Overall, though, I think most tutors would agree that the marking of assignments is a 'justice broadly done' and that we tend to be charitable, rather than miserly, with the marks (Miller and Partlett, 1974: 42), but that doesn't mean there might not be a few biases.

Inconsistency across markers

There have been many studies highlighting inconsistencies across markers. For example, when Bloxham et al. (2015) asked experienced examiners to mark twenty assignments graded as borderline 2:1 (B) or 2:2 (C) by universities, their marks ranged from a first (A) to a third (D)! Nine of the 20 assignments were ranked as both best and worst by different examiners and only one assignment was ranked the same by all examiners (Table 1.2 on page 9 provides an explanation of the UK degree classification system).

But perhaps you should be more concerned about *consistency*. When Garry et al. (2005) compared the marks awarded for 11 essays, they found that 'second markers' (who knew the original mark) generally awarded the same or similar marks (within 3 percentage points), whereas independent markers varied quite significantly: for five of the 11 essays the difference was 9 percentage points or greater. The reason for these results? Well, to put it simply, we have a tendency to 'adjust' and 'anchor' our judgement about something based on a prior judgement, such as the mark awarded by the first marker (though they also point out that it may simply be 'easier' to agree than disagree).

'Hawks' and 'doves' – and other forms of bias in markers

Is your marker a hawk or a dove?

Illustration 1.1

We all know that some tutors are 'harder' markers than others. In medicine, for example, examiners are sometimes referred to as 'hawks' or 'doves': 'hawks' are hard markers who tend to fail candidates (sympathises with the patient – ensuring competent doctors); 'doves' are more lenient examiners (sympathises with the candidate). Studies (Aslett, 2006; Owen et al., 2010) have also suggested other sources of bias in markers based on:

- **Knowledge of student and previous performance**. If a student who normally gets high marks submits a poor assignment, allowances may be made due to the 'halo effect' – which is why many courses use 'anonymous marking' where the identity of the student is not included with the assignment. (The 'halo effect' is discussed in more detail in Chapter 6.)

- **Order/contrast effects**. Several studies have found that the mark awarded to an essay may depend on the quality of those marked before it. If it follows a poor assignment, there's a tendency to award a higher mark, but if it follows a really good assignment, there's a tendency to award a lower mark (Spear, 1997). Though it should be added that the extent to which this actually applies in practice, rather than experimental situations, may be debatable.

- **Physical attractiveness**. Studies have shown that we tend to attribute more favourable character traits to people who are physically attractive, e.g. more intelligent, friendly, or sensitive (Miller, 1970). When Landy and Signall (1974) attached a photograph of an attractive student to an essay, they found it received a higher grade than the same essay with a photograph of an 'unattractive student' or 'no photograph' attached! A case for anonymous marking perhaps?

Study finds attractive students get higher marks

Illustration 1.2

If at first you don't succeed, try again (and again? and again?)

What happens if you fail the assignment? Well, on many courses you may be allowed one resubmission and, assuming that you have no justifiable extenuating/mitigating circumstances (suspicions are raised when the third grandmother dies), this may mean that the highest mark you can get for your resubmission is the minimum pass mark (since it would be unfair to those who passed first time if you were to achieve a higher mark upon resubmission).

Now obviously, failing an assignment is a bit of a disaster, so if you have some anxieties about a piece of coursework make sure that you talk to the tutor *before* submitting the assignment (don't 'bury your head in the sand'). Check what's expected to ensure that you will be addressing the key 'learning outcomes' and assignment guidelines.

For those of you who are really pessimistic, it's also worth checking exactly how many chances you do get to resubmit a piece of work. I know of some courses where students may be allowed up to four attempts at an assignment (that's an initial fail and then three subsequent attempts). After failing at the third attempt the feedback involves an electrical current...

How degrees are classified

For those unfamiliar with the UK university system, the terms 'two-one' and 'two-two' may sound like a foreign language, but they are used to represent a particular class of degree. Table 1.2 provides an outline of the degree classification system, along with the percentage of students in the UK who were awarded each class for the year 2012/13. Notice that 71% of full-time students received a 2:1 or a first. Indeed, many graduate employers require a 2:1 as the minimum standard for entry. Better keep reading this book, eh?

Table 1.2   Degree classification in the UK

Class	Also known as	Represents average of marks for course[1]	Equivalent grade	Percentage of UK full-time students awarded each classification (2013/14)[2]
First-Class Honours	'a first'	70%+	A	20%
Upper Second-Class Honours	'a two-one' (2:1)	60–69%	B	51%
Lower Second-Class Honours	'a two-two' (2:2)	50–59%	C	24%
Third-Class Honours	'a third'	40–49%	D	5%

[1]There may be some discretion for borderline cases.
[2]Higher Education Standards Agency, 2016.

It's important to be aware that, for most universities, it is only the marks from years 2 and 3 that count towards final degree classification, and that these may be weighted, for example, where year 2 counts for 30% but year 3 counts for 70%. The particular system used at your university should be explained in your student handbook; it can vary considerably across institutions: the same profile of marks can produce a different class of degree depending on which university it is (Curran and Volpe, 2004).

Finally, it is worth noting that there has been dissatisfaction with the UK degree classification system for some years now. The main problem is that it's simply not specific enough, especially since the majority of students (70%) are now receiving a first or a 2:1. Think about it: you managed to get an overall grade of 69% but your degree classification is the same as someone who got 60%: a 2:1. You were only one percentage point lower than someone who averaged 70%, but they received a first! Various solutions have been proposed, including providing a more detailed profile of the marks you gain for your modules, and moving to the Grade Point Average (GPA) system used in the USA and widely across the world – which has already been piloted in a number of UK universities. Table 1.3 provides a comparison of the current UK and proposed new GPA system.

Table 1.3 The Grade Point Average scale

Grade	Standard	Grade Point	UK current descriptor
A+	Excellent	4.25	Top first
A	Excellent	4.00	Good first
A-	Excellent	3.75	Low first
B+	Good	3.50	High 2:1
B	Good	3.25	Mid 2:1
B-	Good/satisfactory	3.00	Low 2:1
C+	Satisfactory	2.75	High 2:2
C	Satisfactory	2.50	Mid 2:2
C-	Satisfactory	2.25	Low 2:2
D+	Adequate	2.00	Third
D	Pass	1.00	Low third or pass
D-	Marginal fail	0.50	Marginal fail
F	Fail	0.00	Fail

Source: Higher Education Academy, 2016

From school to college to university: learning to help yourself

The American poet John Ciardi (1916–1986) once quipped that 'a university is what a college becomes when the faculty loses interest in its students'. Now hopefully this isn't the case, but many students do notice a reduction in 'contact time' compared to their experiences at school or college. This is partly because many university tutors are also engaged in research, but also because you are expected to take more responsibility for your own learning. As the Head of Student Satisfaction at Poppleton University recently pointed out in his address to new undergraduates:

> [Y]ou are now embarking on a great adventure, perhaps the greatest adventure of your life. But before you can embark upon that adventure, you must say goodbye to the life you knew before university.

> No longer can you expect to be molly-coddled in the way you were at school and at home. No longer can you expect to be told what to do. No longer can you expect the answers to your questions to be readily available. No longer can you rely upon someone else to help you out. No longer can you expect to

know where you are or what's happening to you or why it's happening to you and where you might go to find any sort of answer.

Now, for the first time in your life, you are on your own. Left to your own devices. In a jungle without a map. At sea without a rudder. Up a creek without a paddle. Totally abandoned. Thrown to the wolves. Hung out to dry. Welcome to higher education at Poppleton.

(L. Taylor, 2009)

Now hopefully, it's not quite as bad as this satirical account of life at the fictional Poppleton University, but you are moving from an environment where you were probably told what to do, how to do it, and when to do it, to a more liberal environment. You're going to have to manage your own time and become more of an independent learner: you need to learn to help yourself. This means attending the lectures (at least some of them) and going away to apply the principles. It means using your initiative. If you don't, you'll become the victim of that terrible slur on students purveyed by some tutors: 's/he needs "spoon-feeding"'. Hopefully these tips will help you to help yourself. As the poet W. B. Yeats (1865–1939) reputedly said: 'Education is not the filling of a bucket, but the lighting of a fire'.

summary

This chapter has provided you with an important insight into the mind-set of your tutors and the marking process at universities. These are things you need to be aware of if you are to become a successful and *strategic learner*; there's more on 'strategic learners' in Chapter 3, but first, let's have a look at an interesting survey...

2

How to impress and how to distress markers

What do tutors look for when they mark assignments? What impresses them and what frustrates them? In this chapter we'll look at the results of a survey which asked tutors to address these two questions. From the survey you'll gain an important insight into what tutors are really looking for when they mark assignments:

- What they like and what they dislike, what impresses them and what annoys them (sources of 'marker distress')

- The most common mistakes witnessed by tutors when marking student assignments

- Some of the most important things you can do in an assignment to improve your mark

- Some of the worst things you can do that will *reduce* your mark

The results of this survey have also been published in the journal *Assessment and Evaluation in Higher Education* (Greasley and Cassidy, 2010).

A survey of tutors

Having spent some time recording my own observations of common problems when marking assignments, I decided that it would be useful to canvass the views of other tutors. Thirty-two tutors (with a health or social science background) responded to an email survey in which they were asked to:

(a) list up to ten things that annoy/disappoint you when marking assignments

(b) list up to ten things that impress you when marking assignments

The survey produced over 200 comments identifying areas of concern. It also yielded 140 comments listing things that impress tutors when they mark assignments. The astute reader will notice that tutors found more to complain about than admire. As one student commented when I brought up the subject in class: 'Is that the survey which shows what a set of miserable, pedantic *@*$@# you all are?'

Tutors find more to complain about than admire...

Illustration 2.1

Anyway, the comments were coded into themes and the tutors were asked to rank them in terms of:

- the most important thing a student can do to improve their assignments
- the worst thing a student can do in an assignment - that will reduce the mark

We'll discuss these in due course, but first, let's see what the most common problems are.

How to *distress* your tutor: the most common problems in assignments

Table 2.1 (on the next page) lists the most frequent problems identified in the survey. Notice that the top three issues relate not so much to *what* is written but *how the assignment is written and presented*. Thus, it wasn't 'failing to answer the question' or 'failing to read the relevant literature' that topped the table – it was problems with language, grammar and expression (1st), referencing (2nd) and presentation (3rd). So if you thought that these were relatively trivial things, think again. You will need to devote some serious time to sorting out these aspects of your assignment if you want a high mark. These are the essential basics of an assignment; it's assumed you'll get them right.

The other issues listed in Table 2.1 will be discussed in more detail throughout the book, but just to give you a flavour of the problem areas, I've listed some of the comments from the survey in the box below the table.

Table 2.1 The most common problems in assignments

Rank	Problem
1st	Poor language, grammar and expression
2nd	Poor referencing
3rd	Poor presentation
4th	Too much description, too little critical analysis
5th	Poor introductions and conclusions
6th	Not following guidelines for presentation and word limits
7th	Poor structure (organisation/use of headings)
8th	Inappropriate use of appendices
9th	Failing to answer the question
10th	Over-use of quotations
11th	Failing to read the relevant literature
12th	Problems with tables and figures

How to distress markers: comments from the survey

Language, grammar and expression

Failing to proofread assignment for typos, spelling mistakes, grammar, etc.

Mixing up 'there', 'their' and 'they're', 'were' and 'where', 'been' and 'being'

No paragraphs, or single-sentence paragraphs

Acronyms used without full explanations being given first

Use of colloquial terms/conversational language (such as didn't/couldn't/isn't/doesn't)

Referencing and references

References that don't appear in the reference list and vice versa

Inaccurate referencing, despite all the guidance available

Using weak references, e.g. Reader's Digest, 9 o'clock news, etc.

Using too many internet references

Presentation

Assignments with no page numbers

Small/illegible fonts (Arial font is often recommended because it is clear)

Text not double-spaced (or at least 1.5 spaced)

Describing rather than analysing/criticising/evaluating

Not providing some sort of critique of or reflection on the work they've read (i.e. assuming that because it's in print it must be 'right')

Poor introductions and conclusions

No clear introduction or salient conclusion to the assignment

New information in the conclusion

Not following guidelines for presentation and word limits

Incomplete front sheet (not putting student number on front page)

Not adhering to the word limit

Poor structure (organisation/use of headings)

Essays that lack structure and seem to hop from one theme to the next at random; no sense of flow, very little (if any) signposting

Using headings for every paragraph

Inappropriate use of appendices

Appendices that are not referred to or discussed in the assignment or have little or no purpose

Failing to answer the question

Writing an abridged version of the essay question on the front page (and then of course failing to answer the question as set)

Overuse of quotations

Too many direct quotes when they should be putting things in their own words

Failing to read the relevant literature

Not using up-to-date references/poor reading round the subject

Not reading widely enough to give a basis for the arguments (or assertions)

Problems with tables and figures

Tables and figures not numbered or discussed

There was also an 'other' category which included some interesting comments about feedback, self-assessment forms, odd smells, and writing in a local accent (see below).

How to distress markers: some other comments from the survey

Feedback

Ignoring feedback given when a draft assignment was submitted

Not learning from the feedback given to previous assignments or to comments on the draft assignment

Most annoying is when they are still making all of these mistakes in semester 2 of year 3!

Perhaps this [survey] will prevent them making the same mistakes over and over!

Self-assessment forms

Utopian self-assessments

Self-assessment forms that say things like 'I know I didn't reference this correctly' or 'I know I didn't follow the guidelines' (really, really annoying)

What's that smell?

My absolute horror - work that smells strongly of tobacco - it makes my office stink

Pages smelling of cigarette smoke!

The paper smelling of either cigarette smoke or some strong perfume. (The latter presumably to lure you into feeling good about the smell so you give them a good mark)

Writing in a local accent (in this case a Yorkshire accent)

Use of 'Yorkshireisms', for example - not recognising words which are supposed to start with an 'H' ('ad' for 'had', etc.)

Students writing 'as' when they mean 'has'

Using 'should of' when they mean 'should have'

Writing 'eee by gum' rather than 'surprisingly'

(OK - I've made this last one up.)

How to *impress* your tutor

So, we've had a taste of what tutors don't like, but what is it that impresses them? Table 2.2 provides the answers.

Table 2.2 What impresses markers?

Rank	What impresses markers
1st	Critical analysis, perspective and argument (with supporting evidence)
2nd	Language, grammar and expression
3rd	Introductions and conclusions
4th	Structure
5th	Presentation
6th	Illustrating and applying ideas to specific contexts
7th	Reading the relevant literature
8th	Following guidelines relating to answering the question and criteria
9th	New information
10th	Referencing and references

From Table 2.2 we can see that what impresses tutors most in an assignment is 'critical analysis, perspective and argument'. This reveals the importance of analysing and evaluating ideas, theories and research studies, rather than simply describing and reporting them.

But notice what came second on the list: 'language, grammar and expression'. This reinforces the importance of devoting a significant amount of time to making sure that your assignment reads well – that the points you are making are communicated clearly and concisely.

Finally, for now, you might notice that referencing came right at the bottom of the list: should we be impressed if the references are all present and correctly formatted according to guidelines, or is this something to be expected?

The box below provides some comments from the survey relating to each of the issues presented in Table 2.2.

How to impress markers: comments from the survey

Critical analysis, perspective and argument (with supporting evidence)

Analysis of reading rather than description

Being aware that just because something is in print this doesn't make it a for-all-time, concrete, unassailable fact!

Ability to see more than one side of an argument

(Continued)

(Continued)

Language, grammar and expression

Clarity of writing making it easy for me to read and follow

Introductions and conclusions

A good introduction that states the aims of the work and a concise conclusion that reflects the introduction and the student's own conclusion

Identifying clearly in the introduction what issues the student is going to investigate

Structure

Clear signposting of ideas that enables the work to flow in a logical manner to a conclusion

Good use of headings and subheadings

Presentation

Paying careful attention to guidelines for the assignment and presentation of work – these are easy marks to gain

That time has been taken to proofread the essay to ensure that there are no typos, etc.

Illustrating and applying ideas to specific contexts

Relating discussion to actual examples

Reading the relevant literature

Evidence of a good range of reading (including texts taking a different perspective) Reading over and above the set texts

Good use of references to support discussion, such as when students cite several authors for one 'statement' showing they have read around and integrated what they have read

Following guidelines relating to answering the question and criteria

Addressing the question – and showing they are answering the question

Reference and thought put into the marking criteria

Including new information

Telling me something I didn't know by going beyond the reading/ lectures

The essay content is different from the others I am marking

Students who tackle the question in a new/original way

Drawing in related learning from other modules, for example, rather than treating each element of learning as separate

Referencing and references

Correct referencing, following guidelines

The most important thing you can do to improve your mark is …

So, we've had a brief look at how to distress and how to impress tutors, but what is it that has the most *positive* and the most *negative* impact on the mark? In Table 2.3 we can see what happened when the tutors ranked each issue in terms of what they felt has the most positive impact on the mark.

Table 2.3 How to improve your mark in assignments

Rank	What has the most positive impact on the mark?
1st	Critical analysis, perspective and argument (with supporting evidence)
2nd	Following guidelines relating to answering the question and criteria
3rd	Illustrating and applying ideas to specific contexts
4th	Structure
5th	Language, grammar and expression
6th	Reading the relevant literature
7th	New information (different, original)
8th	Referencing and references
9th	Introductions and conclusions
10th	Assimilating feedback
11th	Presentation

There are a few key points to take from Table 2.3.

First, the most important element is 'critical analysis, perspective and argument (with supporting evidence)': it wasn't, as you might expect, answering the question (though this was a close second). This shows how highly critical analysis and argument are valued in the minds of tutors.

The second point to note is the importance of 'illustrating and applying ideas to specific contexts'. This is closely related to 'critical analysis, perspective and argument' in terms of grounding the discussion of ideas, theories, etc. in actual examples.

And finally, notice that in seventh place there is a category called 'new information (different, original)'. The provision of 'new information' (beyond that covered in the module) may be an impressive feature in an essay, for example, tackling the question in a way that is different from the other essays – especially, as one tutor commented, 'when you've got a bunch of 150 scripts to mark!' (Though make sure your originality isn't at the expense of answering the question.)

And the worst thing you can do in an assignment is ...

Table 2.4 lists some of the worst things you can do in an assignment – where marks are lost. Not surprisingly, 'failing to answer the question' took the top spot, but look at what came second: poor language, grammar and expression. This might be surprising to some, but what use is a report if it can't be understood?

Notice also, in bronze medal position, 'too much description, too little critical analysis'. It's that phrase 'critical analysis' again. As we shall see, description

Table 2.4 The worst thing you can do in an assignment

Rank	The worst thing you can do in an assignment
1st	Failing to answer the question
2nd	Poor language, grammar and expression
3rd	Too much description, too little critical analysis
4th	Poor structure
5th	Not following guidelines for presentation and word limits
6th	Failing to read the relevant literature
7th	Poor referencing
8th	Poor introductions and conclusions
9th	Inappropriate use of quotations
10th	Poor presentation
11th	Inappropriate use of appendices
12th	Problems with tables and figures

may have been sufficient at school or college, it may even get you through some of the first year at university, but beyond that you will need to start focusing on critical analysis.

Key advice from tutors

In a more recent survey of tutors I asked, 'What key advice (tips) would you give to students about doing essays and assignments?' Their advice highlighted five areas, in the following order of prevalence:

1. Develop your argument

2. Read widely (and critically)

3. Answer the question

4. Plan your assignment

5. Get formative feedback

Unsurprisingly, 'answer the question' figured highly in their comments, but it was interesting to see that 'develop your argument' was the most frequent piece of advice – confirming the results of the original survey. It was also interesting to see their emphasis on reading widely (beyond set texts and resources) and getting formative feedback. I've provided some of their comments in Box 2.1.

box 2.1

Key advice from tutors

Develop your argument

- Take a line of argument. Merely outlining that X said this and Y said this is overly descriptive and fails to develop a critical standpoint, which is what you should be aiming for
- Think about what you want to argue in relation to the question, and structure the assignment around that argument
- Clearly set out the structure of the argument in the introduction, the question that is being asked and how it will be answered. In the conclusion refer back to this and show how it has been answered
- Ensure that the steps in your argument are logical and that these can be traced throughout your essay/assignment
- Plan the essay clearly. Work out what the argument is going to be, the premises of that argument and the empirical evidence that will support the argument

(Continued)

(Continued)

Read widely

- Read widely around the subject area (the reading list is a start – not the end)
- Don't read passively. Read the literature carefully and in a critical way

Answer the question

- Follow the brief and answer the question. Make sure you reference the question throughout and that you provide a clear answer
- Revisit the question and make sure you've answered it
- Answer the question you've been given, not the one you want

Plan your assignment

- Plan your assignment – use headings and sub-headings to help structure it
- Plan it before you write it – draw it out visually on a bit of paper

Get formative feedback

- Think about scheduling and time management – and make sure that you leave yourself time to send drafts or ask for advice. The students who do this with plenty of time to spare *always* get the best marks because I will have told them what they need to do to boost their grades
- Seek tutorial support/guidance (students seem to think they should only do this if they are struggling)

summary

In this chapter you've gained an important insight into the minds of tutors when they mark assignments – what impresses them and what distresses them. You've also been tipped off about the most common mistakes committed by students when writing assignments. So we've laid the foundations, and you've got some pretty good advice already, so now let's get started on the tips.

3

Before you start, some rules of the game

In this chapter we'll take a look at some of the strategies used by the more astute students to gain higher marks for their assignments – in particular, adopting the role of the 'cue-seeker' and taking a 'deep' approach to learning. We'll also examine some so-called 'rules of the game' for writing assignments at university – a catalogue of dubious tactics which some students have used in an attempt to influence the mark they are awarded for their assignments.

Tip 1: How to make the jump from a 2:1 to a first: be a cue-seeker

Are you a cue-seeker? You ought to be. What, you don't know what a 'cue-seeker' is? Well, they've been around a long time in higher education, even if you weren't aware of the label. I used to hang around with a 'cue-seeker' when I was an undergraduate – he got a first (I got a 2:1, being slightly 'cue-deaf'). Let me explain.

A few years ago some research was conducted into the strategies used by students to gain clues about what's required for an assignment – that is, what the tutor is *really* looking for in a good assignment. This has been referred to as a kind of 'hidden agenda' – a set of implicit, unstated rules for achieving a good grade. The problem is that these are often locked away in the minds of tutors. The task of the student is to coax and charm it out of them. With this in mind, Miller and Partlett (1974) identified three types of student:

- The cue-conscious
- The cue-seeker
- The cue-deaf

The cue-conscious are those students who are aware of the 'cues' sent out by tutors – things like picking up hints about exam topics, noticing which aspects of the subject are favoured by the lecturer, whether they are making a good impression in a tutorial, and so on.

Cue-seekers, however, are less passive. They actively seek to extract hints from tutors at every opportunity in order to give themselves the best chance of getting a high grade and a good degree. They adopt a more strategic approach where the aim is to achieve the highest possible grades.

In contrast, cue-deaf students are oblivious to any cues or hints made by tutors. They simply believe that hard work is the ingredient for success. They also believe that the impression they make on tutors – if they make one at all – will not affect the way they are marked.

Now comes the interesting bit. With this typology in mind, Miller and Partlett (1974) asked four independent judges to place a class of 30 students in one of these three categories: cue-seeker, cue-conscious or cue-deaf. They then looked at the degree classification at the end of the course. Table 3.1 provides the results. The majority of cue-seekers got a first, the majority of cue-conscious students got a 2:1, and most cue-deaf students ended up with a 2:2 or a third. One of the cue-seekers made the following comment:

> Everybody does play the game in a sense, everybody's looking for hints, but some of us look for it or probe for it, rather than waiting for it to come passively. We actively go and seek it. (Miller and Partlett, 1974: 60)

Table 3.1 Degree classification for cue-seeker, cue-conscious and cue-deaf students (adapted from Miller and Parlett, 1974)

Degree class	First	2:1	2:2/Third/Ordinary	Totals
Cue-deaf	1	2	11	14
Cue-seekers	3	1	1	5
Cue-conscious	1	6	4	11
Totals	5	9	16	30

Miller and Partlett point out that while cue-seekers admitted to 'playing the game', they were also studying 'extremely hard', and their 'behaviour could equally well be described as an intelligent, adaptive and realistic strategy. Our own impression, from interviewing the cue-seekers, was primarily of their greater maturity in being able to stand outside the assessment situation, to analyse it coolly and to decide how to cope with it' (1974: 69).

Now, you may not want to adopt the strategies of the cue-seeker. You may not need to do it. You may not be so focused on your grade or you may not have the time or the inclination. But if the difference between, for example, a 2:1 and a first is important to you, then getting this 'feedback' can be crucial.

The message here, then, is to seek cues from the tutor about what is required, what is valued in the assignment, for example key issues that should be addressed, types of evidence, areas of focus, and priorities in terms of content. There is nothing wrong with this. In fact, it may help you and the whole class to explore and tease out these issues. Ultimately it will help the tutor also, since when the time comes for marking, the assignments should be more in tune with what s/he is wanting.

Tip 2: Adopt a deep/strategic approach to learning

The problem with some cue-seekers is that they may be accused of adopting what is scathingly referred to in higher education circles as a 'surface approach' to learning. Their primary goal is to complete the task required with little real understanding or exploration of the issues. At worst, they are just memorising and regurgitating a few facts – as the label suggests, just skimming the surface.

What tutors really want is for students to be interested in their subject – to show that they really understand a subject and hopefully have some perspective and point of view on the issues they are discussing. In other words, they are looking for a 'deep approach' to learning (Marton and Säljö, 1976). This can only really come from reading round a subject, exploring it further and, crucially, actually thinking about it. In this respect, it's interesting to note the comment of one student who was asked to record her thoughts about learning and writing assignments at university:

> The more I do think about it, the more convinced I am that what is needed is evidence of your own thinking critically applied to whatever information you've been given, be it Psychology or English or whatever. I should have it engraved on my heart – for every minute spent reading or learning or memorizing, spend ten minutes THINKING. (Norton et al., 2009: 12)

Incidentally, this student went on to graduate with a first-class honours degree.

Which one did you say is taking the 'deep approach' to learning?

Illustration 3.1

Deep learning is about following the references and building up your knowledge in layers – like a good oil painting: the skin on the face of the Mona Lisa isn't one coat of 'flesh pink'. Unfortunately, however, we can only go as deep as time allows, so you will probably need to combine the 'deep' approach with the more cue-seeker-like 'strategic' approach to studying (Entwistle, 2000). Table 3.2 summarises the three approaches to studying: surface, deep and strategic.

Table 3.2 Approaches to studying: surface, deep and strategic

Surface approach	Deep approach	Strategic approach
• Just wants to complete task and meet basic course requirements • Lacks interest in subject (task is an imposition) • Passive reception of information (reproduces information and accepts ideas uncritically) • Doesn't link relevant information from different modules	• Wants to understand – has intrinsic interest in subject • Reads beyond the course requirements • Relates ideas to own knowledge and experience (real life) • Examines evidence and arguments • Links information across different modules	• Wants to achieve highest grade possible • Organises time and study methods effectively • Focuses on assessment criteria and is alert to cues about marking schemes

Tip 3: Know the 'rules of the game': some dubious strategies to gain higher marks

Is writing assignments at university really just about 'playing the game'? Do you think there are certain rules in this game that will help you get a high mark? Well, that's what the results of one study revealed.

Norton et al. (1996) were concerned that the methods of assessment at their university were actually encouraging students to adopt a 'surface' approach to learning (rather than the preferred 'deep approach'). In particular, they suspected that students might be adopting dubious tactics to improve their chances of getting a higher mark for their assignments. They refer to these tactics as 'rules of the game': strategies that tutors may not be aware of, but which students believed would influence their tutors to give the essay a good mark (as opposed to strategies endorsed by tutors).

Seventy second-year psychology students were asked to generate as many of these tactics as they could think of, for example, if they had used them themselves or knew of other students using them. The results make interesting reading for any student (and tutor). They are listed in Table 3.3.

You might recognise some of the tactics listed in Table 3.3 (I've used a couple of them myself in the past), but you might also argue that some of these strategies are surely what tutors would want to encourage? They are certainly included as tips in this book. For example, what's wrong with:

- playing the role of a good student (being keen, enthusiastic, motivated) (ROG 12)?
- using lots of up-to-date, interesting references (ROG 16)?
- including information not covered in the lectures, obscure references (ROG 20)?

The concern is that they are superficial strategies: the student is *playing the role* of being a keen student – it's just an act, or they're just including obscure references for the sake of it. Or perhaps there are more devious motives, as Norton et al. (1996: 159) reveal: 'Some students actually said that the reason why they went for obscure information was to plagiarize it and precisely because it was obscure, they hoped that the tutor would not be able to track it down.'

The slightly worrying aspect to all of this was that when Norton et al. (1996) went on to compare first- and third-year students, they found that the third years admitted to using more of these tactics than the first years. On closer inspection, however, this might simply reflect the wisdom of experience. For example, here are some of the strategies that saw an increase:

- Found out who would mark the essay so that you could choose the title set by the easiest marker, or the tutor you get on best with
- Asked tutor for help so s/he will approve of you and think you're a keen student
- Used up-to-date/interesting references/lots of references
- Tried to include information not covered in the lectures, obscure references
- Avoided putting simple/basic textbooks in the bibliography, even though they have been used
- When feeling confident, argued a position regardless of the tutor's views in order to appear insightful, clever, etc.

Table 3.3 'Rules of the game' (adapted from Norton et al., 1996a and 1996b)

ROG	Tactic
1	Got to know the tutors socially in order to favourably influence them (e.g. by spending time with them outside lectures, asking them about their interests/hobbies/families, having a drink with them)
2	Put your greatest effort into getting a high mark for the first submitted essay in a course (because of the 'halo effect')
3	Made your essay visually exciting (e.g. used 'fancy' designs for headings, pictures/diagrams)

(Continued)

Table 3.3 (Continued)

ROG	Tactic
4	Found out who is marking the essay so you could choose the title set by the easiest marker, or the tutor you get on best with
5	Avoided criticising your marker's views and/or research in the essay
6	Asked tutor for help so s/he will approve of you and think you're a keen student
7	Chosen the easiest title to give you a good chance of getting a high mark
8	Tried to reflect your tutor's opinions/views/style as closely as possible
9	Used big words/technical terms/jargon to impress your tutor
10	Avoided writing anything controversial in the essay
11	Invented studies/research/articles to include in the essay
12	Played the role of the good student (e.g. being keen, enthusiastic, motivated)
13	Acted extra 'nice'/asked for sympathy to get an extension for your essay
14	Chosen an essay title nearest to the tutor's subject or research area
15	Handed the essay in before the deadline to create the impression that the assignment was mastered without difficulty or to show eagerness
16	Used up-to-date/interesting references/lots of references
17	Wrote a lot/used a large font/make the essay look longer, exceed the word limit
18	Chosen a difficult title in the hope of being given extra credit
19	Presented a false bibliography (i.e. one that is long, but you have not consulted all the books on it)
20	Tried to include information not covered in the lectures, obscure references
21	Chosen an unpopular essay title so that your answer is distinctive
22	Changed dates of old research to make it look like up-to-date research
23	Avoided putting simple/basic textbooks in the bibliography even though you have used them
24	When feeling confident, argued a position regardless of your tutor's views in order to appear insightful/clever, etc. [Note: it appears from this that you can't win: either you're reflecting their views (ROG 8) or doing this...]
25	Put a theorist's name against your own point/criticism/comment to make it look erudite
26	Included a false word count
27	Made up false excuse to get an extension for extra time to do a better essay
28	Used abstracts but pretended the actual article had been read
29	Invented references
30	Used previous essay material submitted for a previous course

So, perhaps the fact that more students are adopting these strategies in the third year reflects a learning curve: asking the tutor for help, using up-to-date references, arguing your own position regardless of the tutor's views. In case you're interested, I've added my own comments on each of the strategies in Table 3.4.

Table 3.4 Comments on the 'rules of the game'

Tactic	Comment
Get friendly with tutor (1) Choose easiest marker (4)	Remember that assignments are often second-marked, and then they may go to an external examiner. They may also be 'anonymous'.
Most effort into first essay (2)	This could actually raise expectations. Though it could also produce the 'halo effect' mentioned in Chapter 1 (Box 1.2) and discussed further in Chapter 6.
Make essay visually exciting (3)	Presentation is important, as long as you don't overdo it ('style over substance') and it doesn't detract from the content.
Avoid criticising tutor's views (5) Reflect tutor's views (8) Avoid controversy (10) Argue own position (24)	Criticism should enhance your mark, as long as it's informed (as discussed in Chapters 2 and 8).
Ask tutor for help (6)	If this is a request for formative feedback (though not spoon-feeding) it should go down well (as discussed in Chapter 14).
Choose the easiest title (7) Choose tutor's subject (14) Choose a difficult title (18) Choose unpopular topic (21)	Personally, if there is an option, I'd go for what I'm most interested in. If your interest is supplemented by research, then that should enhance your mark.
Use big words/jargon to impress your tutor (9)	It's important to use the language and terms of the subject, but jargon for the sake of it will probably be a turn-off (see Chapter 9)
Invent studies, articles (11) Invent a false bibliography (19) Change article dates (22) Invent references (25, 29)	You may well be found out – your tutor may be more familiar than you think with the literature. People hate being conned.
Be keen, enthusiastic (12)	Great – as long as it's not just an act.
Act nice to get an extension (13) False excuse for extension (27)	Extensions are unfair to students who submit on time; they can also mess up the tutor's work schedule (and have the opposite effect?). Unless you have a legitimate reason, meet the deadline.
Hand essay in early (15)	It'll just sit in admin till the deadline.
Use lots of up-to-date, interesting references (16)	Good, if relevant and there's evidence you've drawn on them for your assignment.
Make essay longer, exceed word limit (17)	The first will be identified as waffle, the second will be penalised (see Tip 97)
Use obscure references (20)	This is good if it shows you've read widely (as long as it's not a tactic to plagiarise) and they are relevant of course.

(Continued)

Table 3.4   (Continued)

Tactic	Comment
Don't just reference basic textbooks (23) Use abstracts but pretend to have read actual article (28)	A common tactic, I should think, pretending that you've read the journal articles (though it may be reflected in lack of depth in your assignment).
Insert a false word count (26)	If it's noticeably short or long - *compared to the other 50 assignments* - it may be picked up (and easily checked if submitted electronically).
Use material from previous course (30)	Be very careful with this: you can be accused of plagiarising yourself if you resubmit the same work that was produced for another course (see Chapter 11).

'Crafty tactics' - or is it cheating?

Now it's one thing to adopt some 'interesting tactics' when writing your assignments, but quite another to step over the line and 'cheat'. So just in case you're not clear about the dividing line, Table 3.5 provides a list of some behaviours that constitute 'cheating' or, as it is sometimes referred to, 'academic dishonesty'. The list, which was part of a questionnaire study by Newstead et al. (1996), was given to 943 students at a 'large English university' who were asked to indicate whether they had carried out that behaviour at least once or twice during the previous academic year. Needless to say, it was completed anonymously.

Table 3.5 also provides a rating for each of the cheating behaviours: students were asked to rate each item on a scale from 1 (definitely does not constitute cheating) to 7 (definitely constitutes cheating). Since all the mean ratings are above the midpoint of 4, they were all recognised as cheating, though some were obviously regarded as more serious than others.

Table 3.5   Forms of 'cheating' at university and reported occurrence by 943 students at a large UK university (Newstead et al., 1996: 232)

Rank	Cheating or 'academically dishonest behaviours'	% reporting behaviour	Rating
1	Paraphrasing material from another source without acknowledging the original author	54	4.3
2	Inventing data (e.g. entering non-existent results into the database)	48	4.8
3	Allowing own coursework to be copied by another student	46	5.7
4	Fabricating references or a bibliography	44	4.7

Rank	Cheating or 'academically dishonest behaviours'	% reporting behaviour	Rating
5	Copying material for coursework from a book or other publication without acknowledging the source	42	4.5
6	Altering data (e.g. adjusting data to obtain a significant result)	37	5.1
7	Copying another student's coursework with their knowledge	36	5.5
8	Ensuring availability of books/journal articles in the library by deliberately mis-shelving them so that other students cannot find them, or by cutting out the relevant article/chapter	32	4.8
9	In a situation where students mark each other's work, coming to an agreement with another student or students to mark each other's work more generously than it merits	29	5.4
10	Submitting a piece of coursework as an individual piece of work when it has actually been written jointly with another student	18	5.5
11	Doing another student's coursework for them	16	6.2
12	Copying from a neighbour during an examination without them realising	13	6.7
13	Lying about medical or other circumstances to get an extended deadline or exemption from a piece of work	11	5.7
14	Taking unauthorised material into an examination (e.g. cribs)	8	6.8
15	Illicitly gaining advance information about the contents of an examination paper	7	6.5
16	Copying another student's coursework without their knowledge	6	6.9
17	Submitting coursework from an outside source (e.g. a former student offers to sell pre-prepared essays – 'essay banks')	5	6.4
18	Premeditated collusion between two or more students to communicate answers to each other during an examination	5	6.7
19	Lying about medical or other circumstances to get special consideration by examiners (e.g. the Exam board to take a more lenient view of results; extra time to complete the exam)	4	6.1
20	Attempting to obtain special consideration by offering or receiving favours through, for example, bribery, seduction, corruption	2	6.7
21	Taking an examination for someone else or having someone else take an examination for you	1	7.0

Two of the most common behaviours, which were also rated lowest in terms of cheating, were paraphrasing and copying without acknowledging the source (items 1 and 5 in Table 3.5). While paraphrasing without acknowledging the source is certainly not as serious and blatant as some of the other behaviours, it is something that students need to be careful about. Paraphrasing is summarising what someone else has said *in your own words*, and then referencing the source; it's not changing a few words in a passage of text that's been copied from another source (there's an example to illustrate the difference in Chapter 9, Box 9.3). Copying without acknowledging the source is a different matter: it's called plagiarism, it's taken very seriously at universities, and it's the subject of Chapter 11.

According to a recent investigation by the *Independent on Sunday* newspaper (Brady and Dutta, 2012), 45,000 students in 80 higher education institutions were caught cheating over the three-year period to 2011. The offences included taking exams for someone else, using concealed notes in examinations, colluding with other students to produce identical coursework, and paying private firms to write their essays for them (there's more on this in Chapter 11).

summary

If you want to get the most from the classes and the tutors, you should:

- be a cue-seeker – find out what's important, ask questions in the lectures, get some feedback
- adopt a 'deep', rather than 'skimming-the-surface' approach to learning
- be aware of the 'rules of the game' – and that most tutors will be aware of the 'rules of the game'
- be aware of what constitutes 'cheating' – and don't do it! (It's not what you achieve in life, it's how you achieve it.)

So, you've extracted some tips from the tutor and decided to adopt a deep approach to learning. Now you just need to get started …

4

Getting started ... and getting finished

The poet W. H. Auden (1907–1973) said that the 'the aim of education is to induce the largest amount of neurosis that an individual can bear without cracking up' (cited in Omar, 2002). If it feels like that to you sometimes, perhaps you need some tips to help manage your time and your assignments. In this chapter we'll look at some strategies to help you get started with your assignment and keep it focused by having the destination (your conclusion) in mind from the beginning. You'll also find out precisely how long it takes to write a 2,000-word assignment and gain some useful time-management tips.

Tip 4: Develop your argument as early as possible

Your reading needs to be focused on the case you are making, so it's important to map out your assignment and develop your argument as early as possible, perhaps using one or two key sources. Unfortunately, there comes a point when you have to stop reading and researching, gathering material, staring out the window, and start writing the assignment – the sooner the better, some would say: 'It is dangerous to read about a subject before we have thought about it ourselves ... When we read, another person thinks for us; we merely repeat his mental process' (Arthur Schopenhauer (1788–1869), cited in Durant, 1926: 250).

So once you have a grasp of the key issues, start planning and mapping out the essay. A common strategy is to draw a 'mind map' visualising the key sections, topics and issues you'll need to discuss in your assignment. For example, a simple mind map for an assignment about the potential use of acupuncture as a treatment for asthma might look like the one provided in Figure 4.1. It's only after you've begun to map out your assignment in this way that you become aware of the information you'll need to gather.

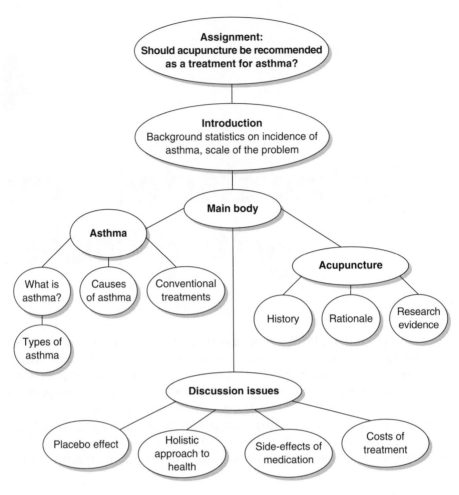

Figure 4.1 A mind map for an assignment

Tip 5: Clever people work backwards: know where you're going before you set off

We'll discuss the importance of conclusions and arguments in more detail later, but for now it's important to emphasise that you should always be clear about your destination before you start writing: what will be your conclusion? It's only once you've decided what your 'destination' will be that you can plan the route. This will help you to focus your reading and research on the relevant information for the case you are making.

How long does it take to write a 2,000-word university essay?

'How long have you got?' is one answer. Some people will use all the time available, others will rattle an assignment off in a couple of days (or less). It depends on the assignment, your interest in the subject and what grade you're aim-ing for. When a student posted this question on the 'studentroom' discussion forum (www.thestudentroom.co.uk), these were some of the replies:

Q: How long does it take to write a 2,000 word university essay?

About a week, maybe a few days more.

Usually, I spend a day doing the research and writing a quick plan, then write the essay itself in about two hours. Of course, that assumes I actually know what research I need to do, and how.

Depends. I've done one in two days before – one for research, the other for writing. On average however I would say 3–5 days, depending on how long I take to research. I usually do the write up in one night.

If it's assessed, I spend far longer than the others who have posted! Probably 5 days for 3500 words

About 6 days doing 4–5 hours a day. Could do it a lot quicker but I always do way more research than I actually need to.

Probably 3 days working reasonably hard at it. Research would take quite a bit longer though.

What!! my last essay, not sure how much i spent on research cus i did it in little bit over a couple of weeks, but the write up took me at least 12 hours! you guys are quick!

Woa...I think I must be spending too much time on essays! O_O

For my last one I did about 15 hours research over 4 days, then write it over about 10 hours. Then again I don't rush at all, I try an take my time with the writing and research in little chunks.

normally 5 days to a week, but the research usually takes a week

I've been working on this one for about 3/4 days researching and i've probably spent 6 hours writing so far and i've done just over half of a 2500 word essay. That said, the referencing takes me ages!

However much time I have. All of it.

If we go by the responses from these students, the time spent on an assignment can be anything from 2–3 *days* to 2–3 *weeks*. If only we knew what marks they each got.

So there's no simple answer. There are, however, some guidelines. For example, Table 4.1 provides an outline of the steps taken to complete an essay, with an indication of how much time each step might take. It all adds up to around 50 hours: about 30 hours of planning, researching and reading, and then a further 20 hours of writing, proofreading and sorting out the references. If that sounds excessive to you, well, it might not to those students who receive an A for their assignments.

Table 4.1 Time spent writing a 2,000-word assignment

Step	Tasks	Start	Time
1	Analyse the question (see Chapter 7) by defining the terms and mind-mapping (see Tip 4). Refer to the learning outcomes to ensure you are covering all the relevant criteria (see Tip 40)	5-7 weeks before due date	2-3 hours
2	Research the topic by consulting the recommended reading and other sources of information (literature search). Read relevant literature, formulate your argument (see Tip 4 and Chapter 8); revise mind map for assignment	4-7 weeks before due date	20-30 hours
3	Write first draft of assignment	2-3 weeks before due date	8-10 hours
4	Revise and edit first draft (see Tip 60 - good writing is achieved through re-writing)	1-2 weeks before due date	6-8 hours
5	Make minor revisions, check references and get someone to proofread your assignment. This is a very important final stage so you should allow sufficient time for this - see Tip 82 (referencing - 'these are easy marks to lose or gain') and Tip 100 (proofreading)	1 week before due date	2-4 hours

Tip 6: How do you eat an elephant? (Slice by slice)

If you're feeling overwhelmed by the scale and scope of an assignment, particularly a longer one such as a dissertation, the way to solve this is to map it out into sections, like the example mind map in Figure 4.1, or perhaps by just putting some headings in place, and then focus on one section at a time.

Tip 7: Work when you work best

I remember talking to a student who was struggling to get her assignments completed due to other commitments in her life (yes, it did end up with a request for an extension). The conversation went something like this:

Me: So when do you work on your assignments?

Student: I start at 11pm.

Me: Aren't you tired?

Student: Yes, I fall asleep...

There's a problem here, and it's partly about the difficulties of doing academic work when you have other commitments, but it's also about time management and taking studying seriously, that is, making sure you have some protected study time, preferably at a time when you work best.

Tip 8: End the day on a 'high'

Personally, when I'm writing something, I like to stop when the going is good. That way, when I return to the work I can start with something easy that doesn't require too much brain power. I'm not the only one, as the writer Haruki Murakami (2008: 5) advises: 'I stop every day right at the point where I feel I can write more. Do that, and the next day's work goes surprisingly smoothly. I think Ernest Hemingway did something like that.'

Tip 9: When the going gets tough, go for a walk

If you're really struggling with an assignment and you're a bit stuck, take a break, go for a walk, do something else and mull it over, rather than staring at the blinking cursor. This can help to clarify what you're thinking and return with a fresh perspective to the problem. The novelist Hilary Mantel suggests a number of other activities, such as baking a pie, as long as you don't just sit there 'scowling at the problem' (*Guardian*, 2010).

Walking in particular has been a favoured activity for writers and philosophers like Virginia Woolf, Friedrich Nietzsche, Thomas Hobbes and Bertrand Russell to stimulate creative ideas; and more recently, innovative thinkers like Steve Jobs (founder of Apple) and Jack Dorsey (founder of Twitter) cited long solitary walks as important tools for thinking. It has been suggested that the creative process involves four phases – preparation, incubation, insight and verification – and that walking is particularly good for the incubation period because it gives the mind an opportunity to relax and lets the unconscious work on the problem, which is essential for insight to appear (Keinänen, 2015). Which reminds me of the famous story about the woodcutter; there are various versions but many can be traced back to Steven Covey's book *The 7 Habits of Highly Effective People* (habit 7 – sharpen the saw):

> Suppose you were to come upon someone in the woods working feverishly to saw down a tree.
>
> "What are you doing?" you ask.
>
> "Can't you see?" comes the impatient reply. "I'm sawing down this tree."
>
> "You look exhausted!" you exclaim. "How long have you been at it?"
>
> "Over five hours," he returns, "and I'm beat! This is hard work."
>
> "Well, why don't you take a break for a few minutes and sharpen that saw?" you inquire. "I'm sure it would go a lot faster."
>
> "I don't have time to sharpen the saw," the man says emphatically. "I'm too busy sawing!"
>
> (Covey, 2004: 287)

Tip 10: Plan your time, get a diary, make a list

Table 4.2   'How I spent my week': typical student

	Monday	Tuesday	Wednesday	Thursday	Friday (essay due 12 noon)
Morning	Jeremy Kyle Show	Can't remember	DNA results (JK Show)	Can't remember	Request extension
Afternoon	Pub	Update *Facebook*	Re-string guitar	Campus finance centre	Sack life coach
Evening	Party	Pub	Party	Pub	Party

If your week looks anything like Table 4.2 you may need to rethink how you are managing your time.

Time management is about planning and prioritising. You can do this by:

- drawing up a plan, perhaps in the form of Table 4.2 (not the contents, of course)
- writing a list of 'things to do today'

But without wishing to state the obvious, the main thing is to get on with what you need to do in a focused way: to plan your time more efficiently. In this respect, the following account might be instructive.

In 1963 the Beatles' Paul McCartney moved in with the actress Jane Asher at her family's large house on Wimpole Street, London. The family had a very structured timetable.

> Paul: The whole style of the family influenced me because of this social diary they kept. The idea that the whole day was planned was fascinating for me. They were the first people I knew that would literally have from seven in the morning till late at night in a diary, laid out … It could be like nine o'clock so-and-so, five minutes past nine, telephone so-and-so. I've never known people who stuffed so much into a day. … I was amazed by the diary. It did actually structure me a lot. It makes things easier, you can think through the problem in hand and not be bothered by every other peripheral thing. (Miles, 1998: 114–15)

So draw up a list, structure your time and get yourself a diary. (Welcome to the middle class.)

If you would like some more time-management tips, there's lots of it about on the internet. Perhaps your first port of call should be the Learnhigher website (www.learnhigher.ac.uk), which provides advice on things like planning your time (drawing up weekly timetables, termly timetables, project timetables), working more effectively, and prioritising tasks. There's also a list of the 'top ten distractions' that students face when studying (e.g. emails, Facebook, computer games, family, housework), along with some ideas about how to deal with them. For example, fix a time to look at email and phone messages or work in the library to avoid distractions at home. And when it comes to house-work, the message seems to be to lower your standards: leave the ironing, and clean the cooker when you've graduated.

. If you really like structuring your time with weekly timetables such as the one in Table 4.2, you could even produce a Gantt chart scheduling your activ-ities week by week, such as the examples provided in Figures 4.2 and 4.3. And once you've done all this planning and timetabling and working out how many hours in the week you've got to do all the things you need to do, you can work out how much you could have got done if you'd not spent all this time plan-ning. If only things were so predictable.

Activities	Weeks											
	1	2	3	4	5	6	7	8	9	10	11	12
Receive assignment question	▓											
Research/obtain references		▓	▓									
Reading		▓	▓	▓	▓							
First draft						▓	▓					
Revise draft								▓	▓			
Proofread										▓		
Check references											▓	
Print/hand in												▓

Figure 4.2 Gantt chart planning assignment activities: how it should happen

Activities	Weeks											
	1	2	3	4	5	6	7	8	9	10	11	12
Receive assignment question	▓											
Research/obtain references												▓
Reading												▓
First draft												▓
Revise draft												▓
Proofread												▓
Check references												▓
Print/hand in												▓

Figure 4.3 Gantt chart planning assignment activities: how it really happens

Tip 11: 'Work expands so as to fill the time available for its completion'

This is what's known as 'Parkinson's law'. It's what may happen if you fail to follow the advice in the previous tip, as the following account illustrates:

> It is a commonplace observation that work expands so as to fill the time available for its completion. Thus, an elderly lady of leisure can spend an entire day in writing and dispatching a postcard to her niece at Bognor Regis. An hour will be spent in finding the postcard, another in hunting for spectacles, half-an-hour in a search for the address, an hour and a quarter in composition, and twenty minutes in deciding whether or not to take an umbrella when going to the pillar-box in the next street. The total effort which would occupy a busy man for three minutes all told may in this fashion leave another person prostrate after a day of doubt, anxiety and toil. (Parkinson, 1955)

Hence the saying: 'If you want something done, ask a busy person'.

Tip 12: 'Talent develops in quiet places'

… according to the German writer Goethe, and 'hell is other people' according to the existential philosopher Jean-Paul Sartre. So switch off the mobile, and just check your emails once or twice a day, otherwise you'll be blown off course with every (albeit welcome) distraction.

Tip 13: Submit your assignment at the last minute – and go down a grade?

When David Arnott and Scott Dacko reviewed online submissions from 777 marketing students they found that the mark they received reduced as it got closer to the deadline. Students who submitted at the last minute (literally) lost an average 5 percentage points, taking them down a grade, from a 2:1 to a 2:2 (see Figure 4.4) This is not, of course, surprising: if you're submitting at the last minute you've probably only just completed the assignment – at the last minute.

And whilst it's easy for tutors to tell students that they need to improve their time management (don't we all?), the issue that would concern me is that a good assignment benefits from a little bit of 'sitting time': ideally, leave it for a day or two and then go back and have another look at it. This reflective, reviewing stage can make a significant difference to the finished work – when either you, or ideally someone else, has another look at it and notices grammatical errors, referencing problems and things that aren't quite clear. Tutors don't like stuff that looks like it's been slapped together at the last minute (would you like it if your meal was thrown onto the plate?).

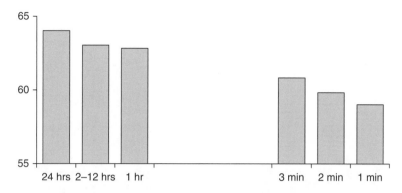

Figure 4.4 Time of submission and average mark (adapted from Arnott & Dacko, 2014)

summary

In this chapter we've looked at some strategies for getting started with your assignment and structuring your time more generally. We've seen the importance of:

- developing your argument as early as possible so that you can focus your reading on what's important and relevant (perhaps using a mind map to highlight the key sections and information you'll need to discuss)
- deciding on your destination/conclusion so that you can plan your route towards it (a kind of backward planning)
- putting the hours in (which is what students who receive a high mark do – even if they may give the impression that they don't)
- breaking the assignment into manageable chunks of work and focusing on one 'bite' at a time
- structuring your time (planning and prioritising) and not succumbing to welcome distractions that need your urgent attention, like re-stringing the guitar, getting to the next level of Grand Theft Auto, and going online to check if that last pair of Doc Martens you bought are also available in black.

5

Reading and researching the literature

Most of the learning that happens at university is achieved by you – the student. We're just there to facilitate learning – and provide some feedback. Unfortunately, for some students at least, this means researching and reading the literature. And that doesn't mean a quick look at Wikipedia.

In this chapter we'll look at the importance of exploring the literature and taking account of different perspectives (being aware that just because something is in print doesn't necessarily mean it's true), along with some advice about the kinds of references you should be citing in your assignment.

Tip 14: **One thing leads to another**

This is not a tip about amorous liaisons; rather it's about the process of reading and researching for an assignment. If you're doing it right, one thing should lead to another. That is, you might start with (heaven forbid) Wikipedia, or perhaps a general textbook, and then follow the references to other sources of literature. It's called research and it's like conducting an investigation, digging deeper and deeper into the literature.

When I used to write assignments I would often spend the day on a tangent: having read one article, the references would lead me to another, and then that would lead to another, and so on, until I found myself in another place completely. As the following comments from the survey (see Chapter 2) show, this is a good thing (if you have the time). It shows that you're adopting the role of the explorer (Chapter 1), venturing beyond the set texts (and in doing so you may be able to impress the tutor by telling them something they didn't know – Tip 21).

What tutors like

- Reading widely and using the literature to develop a critical argument
- A good, broad range of quality references that are appropriately employed and correctly cited
- Demonstrating wide, detailed reading around the subject
- Evidence of a good range of reading (including texts taking a different perspective)
- Reading over and above the set texts
- Use and critique of appropriate reference resources that demonstrate a thorough literature search
- Well-referenced points
- Good use of references to support discussion such as when students cite several authors for one 'statement', showing they have read around and integrated what they have read

What tutors dislike

- Failing to engage with literature
- Not reading widely enough to give a basis for the arguments (or assertions)
- Reliance on only one or two reference sources
- Poor reading round the subject and not using up-to-date references

Tip 15: Use up-to-date references

Obtaining up-to-date references can be crucial for a good mark. I recall marking one assignment discussing the evidence for homeopathy (an 'alternative therapy') and it failed to discuss or reference the most recent review of the evidence, which I had, incidentally, highlighted in the lectures. This oversight significantly reduced my impression of the assignment, and the mark, which was largely justified: here was a key reference that had been ignored. This also highlights the importance of conducting a literature search (see Tip 22).

The most up-to-date articles will be in journals, and it's worth checking whether such articles are available in a preprint electronic version, since journal articles can actually take a while before they become available in print. For example, it took over two years to publish the results of the survey upon which this book is based (Greasley and Cassidy, 2010). Now obviously, this depends on the article and the journal. If the title is 'A cheap and simple cure for all known diseases' or 'Cold fusion repeatedly demonstrated', it may only take a few months for it to appear in print. But if it's 'Injuries due to falling coconuts', or 'Pigeons' discrimination of paintings by Monet and Picasso', you could be waiting a while. (These are actual articles – the former appeared in the *Journal of Trauma* and the latter appeared in the *Journal of the Experimental Analysis of Behavior*.)

Tip 16: Avoid dodgy sources

The source of your references may be crucial to the reliability of the information you are providing in your assignment. For example, I remember reading an essay evaluating the evidence for acupuncture in which the main reference was from *Acupuncture Today* (a 'trade' magazine) – which is not necessarily the most objective and unbiased source of information. It's a bit like citing *Flying Saucer Review* for evidence of UFOs.

It's not surprising, then, that 'poor-quality references' was an issue raised in the survey of tutors.

What tutors dislike

- Using weak references, e.g. Reader's Digest, 9 o'clock news
- Not using original sources, e.g. Doctor on the video shown in the lecture talking about his research [rather than a published source of information]
- Citing the *Sun* newspaper as the main source of evidence for whether a therapy works!

Imagine if the assignment preceding yours has been citing original articles from the *Lancet*, the *British Medical Journal*, the *Quarterly Journal of Experimental Psychology* and the *Harvard Law Review*, and all you've got to offer is the *Sun*, *Wikipedia* and 'the video shown in the lecture'. It's not going to look good, is it?

Tip 17: www.usesparingly.com

The increasing use and reliance on references from the Web was another source of marker distress. Here are a few comments.

What tutors dislike

- Using too many internet references

- Internet reference sources – a small number may be OK, particularly when they come from reputable sources, however copious unrecognised sources will not do

- Non-existent web addresses on the references list [markers do sometimes check the web references – especially if they look dodgy]

Perhaps the key word in the above comments is 'reputable': synonyms include 'of good reputation', 'highly regarded', 'trustworthy'; antonyms might include 'dubious', 'biased' or 'dodgy'. The problem is one of quality assurance. Unlike articles in journals, there is no peer-review process (where other academics review the quality of the article prior to acceptance).

There is no doubt that the internet is a wonderful tool – information at your finger tips – but you need to be selective. Aside from dubious websites promoting their own agendas (e.g. alternative remedies that will cure all ills), some people purposely enter false information, on Wikipedia, for example.

Tip 18: Wikipedia: cite it at your peril?

Wikipedia, the online encyclopaedia, is one of the most popular sites on the web – the seventh most visited site, according to web information service Alexa. And no wonder, it contains over 10 million articles, nearly 3 million in English, covering virtually everything you would ever need to know as a student. But you already know this. Surveys suggest that most students consult Wikipedia when writing assignments. For example, a survey of Cambridge University students reported that over 75% 'had used Wikipedia for researching essays'. But you are probably also aware that most tutors discourage the use of Wikipedia – especially citing it as a primary source.

So what's wrong with using Wikipedia? Why do tutors have such a problem with it? Well, aside from the fact that Wikipedia is a secondary source of information (a second-hand summary of original research reported elsewhere), the primary concern is the reliability of the information, since anyone with access to the internet can contribute and edit the contents. So there are justifiable concerns about the quality of the information contained on the site – its accuracy, validity and objectivity, all of which are key criteria in assignments.

It is for this reason that one academic department proposed a 'wiki ban' on students. In 2007, tutors in the history department at Middlebury College in the USA voted to bar students from citing Wikipedia in their assignments. While a ban was not enforced (or enforceable), the head of the department warned that Wikipedia is not an appropriate source for citations: 'The important point that we wish to communicate to all students taking courses and submitting work in our department in the future is that they cite Wikipedia at their peril' (Jaschik, 2007).

How unreliable is Wikipedia? In 2005 the highly respected British journal *Nature* asked expert reviewers to check the accuracy of information in a range of scientific articles on Wikipedia and compare this to articles in the *Encyclopaedia Britannica* (a more established source of information). They reviewed 42 entries and reported:

> Only eight serious errors, such as misinterpretations of important concepts, were detected in the pairs of articles reviewed, four from each encyclopedia. But reviewers also found many factual errors, omissions or misleading statements: 162 and 123 in Wikipedia and Britannica, respectively. (Giles, 2005: 901)

So, in terms of accuracy, it would appear that Wikipedia is nearly as reliable as the well established and generally respected *Encyclopaedia Britannica* (although the reviewers did report concerns about the 'readability' of some articles which were poorly structured and confusing). But that's still, on average, four errors per article (162 errors in 42 articles).

Perhaps the sensible advice would be to consult Wikipedia as a convenient initial source of information and use the links provided, but not to cite it. The same advice would be given for citing any encyclopaedia. Use it as an initial source of information but try to consult and reference original sources or reputable textbooks.

Tip 19: Make the move to journals as soon as you can

What should you be reading and what should you be citing in your assignment? Well, you might start with general textbooks in your first year and then begin to include more specialised sources like journals in your second and third years, but this does depend to some extent on the academic discipline. For more classical subjects in the arts and humanities, the relevant literature may be more book-based, but for scientific subjects where the evidence is constantly updated, you will need to consult the academic journals which contain the most up-to-date literature.

So while a good textbook is excellent for general information, providing an overview of the subject, as you progress through the years you should be consulting and referencing journal articles more and more, as the following reflection from a student illustrates:

> I think it was learning the research skills. I didn't know how to research really and you pick that up as you go along using the libraries and journals. In the

first year I tended to get a lot of the information from books and also search-ing other areas like the internet. I was getting Cs. In the second and third year I started to go beyond that and started to use journals. [And then her grades started to improve.] (Norton et al., 2009: 28)

We've already noted that the information from journals should be more up to date than that found in books (which can take a few years to write). It may also be more reliable due to the peer-review process.

When an article is submitted to a journal it will be sent out to (typically) three academics with some expertise in the area to 'referee' or 'review' it, that is, to appraise the design of the study, note any errors, suggest improvements, etc. Once the article has been reviewed, the journal editor will write to the author(s) with recommendations about what needs changing for the article to be accepted in the journal (or not accepted, as the case may be). Most recom-mendations are along the following lines:

- Accept without changes (rare – especially if you've got three academics pick-ing at every word)

- Accept with minor revisions (corrections, clarifications, etc.)

- Reject but invite resubmission with major revisions (e.g. rewrite, collect more data)

- Reject outright (fundamentally flawed, or it could be that the article is not appropriate for that particular journal)

So the peer-review process helps to ensure a level of 'quality control'.

Tip 20: **You can get any rubbish published**

Articles in journals may have been through the 'peer review' process, but you should still remember that 'peer review' only means that the paper has been critically evaluated by two or three other academics. The review process is usually anonymous and quite a good means of quality control, but it certainly doesn't mean that the content of the article is 'the truth'. It just means that the article has been through a process to try to maintain standards.

You should also be aware that standards vary across journals. The 'top' journals, such as *Nature* and the *British Medical Journal*, only publish about 5% of submitted articles. The acceptance rate for many other journals, how-ever, can be much higher. So you need to be mindful of the hierarchy of quality across different journals. As the former editor of the *British Medical Journal* once commented: 'You can get any rubbish published, just go down and down and down and down the food chain [of medical journals]' (Fister, 2004: 923).

Although this quote refers particularly to medical journals, the same princi-ple applies in most academic subjects: the top journals in your subject area will usually contain the most important and more rigorously conducted studies, but there will be journals where the standards are less rigorous. As the deputy editor of the *Journal of the American Medical Association*, Drummond Rennie, once commented:

> There seems to be no study too fragmented, no hypothesis too trivial, no literature too biased or too egotistical, no design too warped, no methodology too bungled, no presentation of results too inaccurate, too obscure, and too contradictory, no analysis too self-serving, no argument too circular, no conclusions too trifling or too unjustified, and no grammar and syntax too offensive for a paper to end up in print. (Cited in Smith, 2009)

This is a very important message to remember: journals may be a good source of information, but that doesn't mean you should accept what they say without question, even if they are subject to peer-review:

> Editors and scientists alike insist on the pivotal importance of peer review. We portray peer review to the public as a quasi-sacred process that helps to make science our most objective truth teller. But we know that the system of peer review is biased, unjust, unaccountable, incomplete, easily fixed, often insulting, usually ignorant, occasionally foolish, and frequently wrong. (Richard Horton, editor of the *Lancet*, cited in Horton, 2000: 148)

Remember, no study is perfect, and the authors will usually be requested to present their own list of limitations at the end of the study, all of which reinforces the importance of appraisal skills when reading journal articles. (We will be discussing critical appraisal in Chapter 8.) As an interesting aside, Box 5.1 provides an example of 'the rubbish' that can actually appear in a journal.

box 5.1

Sokal's hoax journal article

In 1996, Alan Sokal, a professor of physics at New York University, sent an article to the American cultural studies journal *Social Text*. The article, entitled 'Transgressing the boundaries: toward a transformative hermeneutics of quantum gravity', was submitted as an 'experiment' to see if a leading North American journal of cultural studies would 'publish an article liberally salted with nonsense if (a) it sounded good and (b) it flattered the editors' ideological preconceptions' (Sokal, 1996b: 62).

When the article duly appeared in the spring/summer 1996 issue of *Social Text* (Sokal, 1996a), Sokal announced that it was intended as a hoax, full of meaningless sentences and nonsensical quotations about physics and mathematics produced by prominent French and American intellectuals. For example:

In the second paragraph I declare, without the slightest evidence or argument, that 'physical reality' [note the scare quotes] ... is at bottom a social and linguistic construct. Not our *theories* of physical reality, mind you, but the reality itself. Fair enough: anyone who believes that the laws of physics are mere social conventions is invited to try transgressing those conventions from the windows of my apartment. (I live on the twenty-first floor.) (Sokal, 1996b: 62)

For a detailed account of the hoax see Sokal and Bricmont (1998) or Sokal's webpage: http://www.physics.nyu.edu/sokal/ (accessed September 2010).

Tip 21: 'Tell me something I don't know'

Some students are not very adventurous – they don't stray beyond the confines of what is covered in the lectures. Perhaps this reflects lack of time, but an assignment which simply regurgitates what was covered in the lectures is not flattering, it's disappointing. The lectures should be seen as the start of your reading and investigation, not the end. Obviously you will need to do the essential reading that has been recommended for your assignment, but as the comments from the survey illustrate, if you really want to impress your tutor, try going beyond the set texts and 'thinking out of the box'.

How to impress tutors

- Telling me something I didn't know by going beyond the reading/lectures
- When I actually learn something from what I've read
- Students who tackle the question in a new/original way
- Thinking out of the box ... occasionally you do get a very well written, meticulously researched and highly polished piece of work that either subverts the question or deals with it in an unusual, but pertinent way. Nice when that happens. Especially if you've got a bunch of 150 scripts to mark!

So try to tell the tutor something they don't know and tackle the question in a different or original way (though make sure you follow the guidelines and meet the learning outcomes, of course).

Tip 22: Do a literature search

Although you should be provided with a list of essential and recommended reading, a further search of the literature identifying other good sources of information will usually impress tutors. As we've noted, students who receive the higher marks will usually delve further into the literature, exhibiting the 'deeper' approach to learning.

You might start with a search on the internet. Google Scholar, for example, will provide you with an indication of what's been published in academic journals, along with links to relevant citations, but if you want reliable academic sources use your library's online subject databases. In Table 5.1, I've listed some of the common databases in my own subject area, the social and health sciences.

Table 5.1 Some common literature review databases

Subject	Database
Health	**AMED** (Allied and Complementary Medicine Database)
	Includes: physiotherapy, occupational therapy, rehabilitation, palliative care and complementary medicine
	CINAHL (Cumulative Index to Nursing & Allied Health)
	Nursing and allied health
	Cochrane
	Database of systematic reviews for health interventions
	PubMed
	PubMed comprises more than 24 million citations for biomedical literature from MEDLINE, life science journals, and online books. Citations may include links to full-text content from PubMed Central and publisher websites
Social sciences	**ASSIA** (Applied Social Sciences Index and Abstracts)
	Health, social services, economics, politics, race relations and education
Psychology	**Psychinfo**
	Psychology (journals from 1887 to the present)
Business and Management	**Proquest**
	Business and management

Techniques for searching the literature within these databases vary, so you will need to consult the relevant guides provided by your university library (which may also offer training in the use of electronic resources), but they generally share the following principles:

1. **Select the appropriate database** for your search, e.g. Medline for medical topics, Psychinfo for psychological topics. (Note: it may be possible to search across several databases at the same time, avoiding the need to repeat your search strategy across individual databases.)

2. **Identify the key words/terms** for your search, e.g. 'acupuncture' and 'pain'.

3. **Use 'filters' to restrict and focus** the literature retrieved, e.g. dates, context. You can also ask it just to search for literature reviews on some databases. This can be a good start if you find one that's recent.

4. **Keep a record** of your literature search by saving the search. Aside from saving you repeating the search at another time, this might be useful to put in an appendix if your assignment warrants it (e.g. if it's a research proposal).

For example, a search of the literature on 'acupuncture' and 'pain' might proceed as shown in Table 5.2. The aim is to reduce the number of 'hits' to a manageable amount. At step 4, I could have filtered by a more recent year of publication to reduce the 'hits' to a manageable amount (publications since 2006), but instead I chose to have a look for any recent literature reviews – which is usually a good start.

Table 5.2 Narrowing down a literature search

Step	Search	Results
1	Search term: 'acupuncture'	= 2,000 hits
2	Search term: 'pain'	= 4,000 hits
3	Combine 'acupuncture' and 'pain'	= 400 hits
4	Filter by year of publication (studies published since 2000)	= 200 hits
5	Restrict to literature reviews only	= 10 hits

For larger assignments, like dissertations or postgraduate research projects, you may be required to conduct a more thorough review of the literature. Indeed, conducting a literature review may be the assignment itself. Chapter 16 provides more detailed guidelines about how to conduct a systematic literature review.

summary

In this chapter we've seen the importance of:

- using up-to-date references – especially for subjects where the knowledge base is updated regularly through new research (e.g. health interventions)
- citing reputable sources (e.g. peer-reviewed articles in good journals)
- being aware that just because something has been published in a book or a journal doesn't mean it's 'the truth' (reliable, beyond criticism, etc.)

(Continued)

(Continued)

- obtaining different perspectives from different sources
- going beyond the recommended reading and perhaps tackling the assignment in a different or original way (telling the marker something they don't already know)
- doing a literature search

So, you've read the relevant literature and identified some interesting information. Now you just need to start working backwards ...

6

Introductions, conclusions and structure

Introductions

As we all know, essays should have a beginning (introduction), a middle (main section) and an end (conclusion). Basically, you tell the reader what you are going to say, say it, and then tell the reader what you've said. In this chapter we'll look at each of these elements, along with more general issues about structuring assignments.

And that was the sum total of my original introduction to this chapter – the problem being that it's too short, which is a common problem in assignments. The trouble is that most people, me included, don't like wasting time (and words) going over what we are going to say; it's tedious – we'd rather just get on with it. But as we'll see in this chapter, a good introduction may be more important than you think when it comes to writing assignments. So let's have another go.

Introductions (second attempt) ...

As we all know, essays should have a beginning (introduction), a middle (main section) and an end (conclusion). Basically, you tell the reader what you are going to say, say it, and then tell the reader what you've said. What could be simpler? Well, if it is that simple, why did issues relating to structure, introductions and conclusions feature so highly on the list of things that frustrate and impress tutors? In this chapter we'll be discussing each of these elements: introductions, conclusions, and then more general issues about structuring assignments.

First, we'll see that a good introduction is crucial for an assignment – providing an outline and overview of the contents, and signposting the route you've taken to address the question (a planned itinerary rather than a mystery tour). We'll also look at *five key criteria* for an effective introduction, proposed by Townsend et al. (1993), which were shown to improve the grade of an assignment.

Next we'll look at three key criteria for a good conclusion, along with an interesting tip about when to write it (not at the end). And finally, we'll examine some tips for maintaining a clear, logical structure to your assignment, using headings and subheadings along with signposting throughout to help the marker on their journey.

It is concluded that paying attention to your introductions and conclusions may be especially important in assignments due to the psychological impact of first and last impressions – which may have a significant influence on markers.

There, so much better, don't you think? I've provided a clearer outline of the contents, added a couple of sentences in the first paragraph justifying the discussion of introductions, conclusions and structure (because they featured as common problems in the survey of tutors) and I've also added a few details about the conclusion.

Tip 23: **Use signposting**

When markers pick up an assignment they often have very little idea of what's in store for them. A good introduction can resolve this problem in a few lines by stating the aims of the assignment and providing a brief outline of the content and argument. It gives the reader a map of where they are going to be taken on the essay journey. In contrast, an essay without an introduction is a bit like a mystery tour – no one has a clue where they are going. So a good introduction shows that you've thought about the itinerary and planned the route.

Not surprisingly, then, the main source of marker distress in the survey of tutors was failing to provide a simple outline or overview of the essay.

What tutors dislike

- Failing to provide a simple introduction and outline of the subject (what is this essay about?)

- Poor introductions which give little overview of the assignment and what to expect

- Not introducing to the reader the content of the assignment or the context

- Not stating the aim of the essay

If you want to impress the marker you should provide a clear introduction that outlines the content, as the following comments illustrate:

What tutors like

- A clear introduction that presages a clear structure
- Good introduction summarising the assignment
- Identifying clearly in the introduction what issues the student is going to investigate

Clearly, it is a good strategy to summarise what you are going to say, with some signposting indicating the route and the directions you will be taking. This is what the introduction to this chapter did – at the second attempt.

Five key criteria for a good introduction: how to move up a grade

A study by Townsend et al. (1993), published in the *Journal of Educational Psychology*, examined a range of essay-writing guides and arrived at five key criteria for an effective introduction. A good introduction for an essay should:

1. Discuss the importance or timeliness of the topic
2. State the problem to be addressed
3. Indicate the scope of the essay
4. Define the terms to be used
5. Delineate the argument to be presented

What makes this study more interesting is that the researchers used these criteria to alter the introductions in some students' essays and found that the marks awarded rose by one grade (see Box 6.1).

box 6.1

An introduction proven to increase your grade

When Townsend et al. (1993) removed the original introductions from student essays, and substituted the following introduction constructed using the five key criteria, the grade increased on average from a B to a B+.

(Continued)

(Continued)

Essay Question: Discuss the role of genetic and environmental factors in IQ scores.

'Geniuses are born not made!' Is it really that simple? The 'nature vs nurture' dispute, in relation to intelligence, remains unresolved. In an attempt to separate the influence of genetic and environmental factors, two kinds of investigation have been important - twin studies and adoption studies. This research has shown that both genetic and environmental factors interact with each other to determine an individual's IQ score. The evidence presented in this essay indicates that IQ is shaped by many influences. In the context of current concerns about the validity of intelligence testing, an understanding of these influences is essential.

This is a good introduction because it:

1   Opens with a common belief about the subject which sets up the debate to be examined and questioned
2   Points out that this is an issue which remains unresolved (the problem to be addressed)
3   Delineates the scope/content to be discussed - evidence from twin and adoption studies
4   Indicates the outcomes of this research and the argument/conclusion in the essay (that IQ is shaped by an interaction between genetic and environmental factors)
5   Concludes by putting the debate into a context - concerns about the validity of intelligence testing (importance/timeliness of the topic)

Why might a good introduction like the one in Box 6.1 make such a positive impact on the grade? Because when you provide an overview of the assignment in this way it helps the marker to understand the relevance of what follows; it contextualises and frames the assignment, and facilitates comprehension.

Bearing this point in mind, try to work out what the following passage is about:

The procedure is actually quite simple. First, you arrange things into two different groups. Of course, one pile may be sufficient depending on how much there is to do. If you have to go somewhere else due to lack of facilities, that is the next step; otherwise you are pretty well set. It is important not to overdo things. That is, it is better to do fewer things at once than too many. In the short run this might not seem important, but complications can easily arise. A mistake can be expensive as well. At first the whole procedure will seem complicated. Soon, however, it will become just another facet of life. It is difficult to foresee an end to the necessity for this task in the immediate future, but then one can never tell. After the procedure is completed, one arranges the material into different groups again. Then they can be put into their appropriate places. Eventually they will be used once more, and the whole cycle will have to be repeated. However, that is part of life.

Did it make sense? Struggling? What about the next passage:

A newspaper is better than a magazine. A seashore is a better place than the street. At first it is better to run than to walk. You may have to try several times. It takes some skill, but it is easy to learn. Even young children can enjoy it. Once successful, complications are minimal. Birds seldom get too close. Rain, however, soaks in very fast. Too many people doing the same thing can also cause problems. One needs lots of room. If there are no complications, it can be very peaceful. A rock will serve as an anchor. If things break loose from it, however, you will not get a second chance.

Just as bad? Just as frustrating? Well, perhaps it would make sense if you knew that the first passage was about washing clothes and the second was about making a kite. And that was the point of John Bransford and Marcia Johnson's experiment from 1972 when they presented these passages to people with or without this contextual information: readers required some knowledge of the topic in order to facilitate comprehension.

While these are quite extreme examples, I think they illustrate the point quite well: you need to signpost and guide the reader/marker through the relevance of what you are saying. This will help them to read it and mark it.

The 'halo effect' and 'confirmation bias'

It is important to note, in this respect, the famous 'halo effect', where our judgements about a person are influenced by a favourable or unfavourable first impression (e.g. Nisbett and Wilson, 1977). A good first impression, at a job interview, for example (smart, friendly), might create a positive feeling towards the candidate, minimising the impact of any subsequent gaffes. A poor first impression, on the other hand, can have the opposite effect – finding fault, etc. – which is known as 'reverse halo effect' (or 'devil effect'). In terms of assignments, then, it may be that a well-written introduction creates a 'halo effect', favourably disposing the marker to the assignment; a poor introduction, on the other hand, may have the opposite effect. Although it could also be that the quality of the introduction simply reflects the quality of the rest of the assignment. In the words of an old Japanese saying, 'One instance shows the rest'.

Studies have also shown that we tend to seek out information that confirms our views and beliefs. This is known as 'confirmation bias' (Nickerson, 1998; Shermer, 2002). For example, if you believe in astrology, and you know the supposed personality traits associated with the different star signs, then you'll tend to look for confirmation in the people you know. Your Taurean friend actually is quite stubborn and bullish. But isn't everyone at times? Aren't they also quite indecisive at times, like Librans, or inquisitive, like Geminis? Confirmation bias means you'll tend to find what you're looking for.

One instance shows the rest...?

Illustration 6.1

How might this apply to the marking of an assignment? Well, if it starts with a good first impression from the opening introduction, then the marker might be predisposed towards focusing on those aspects that confirm this initial positive impression. Conversely, a poor first impression might bias them towards focusing on any errors and inadequacies. As the philosopher Francis Bacon (1561–1626) recognised many years ago:

> The human understanding when it has once adopted an opinion ... draws all things else to support and agree with it. And though there be a greater number and weight of instances to be found on the other side, yet these it either neglects and despises, or else by some distinction sets aside and rejects. (Cited in Shermer, 2002: 296)

A good introduction and a less good introduction: two examples

Bearing all this advice in mind, Box 6.2 provides an example of a very good introduction. It is taken from an assignment written by a second-year student, which received a very high mark. As the comments after each paragraph show, this introduction meets most of the criteria suggested for a good introduction:

1. **Importance and timeliness of the topic (criterion 1) along with the problem to be addressed (criterion 2).** National statistics are provided, stating the scale of the problem, and local statistics indicate relevance for the

local context – also justifying the need to consider new treatments (like acupuncture).

2. **The scope of the essay (criterion 3) and the argument to be presented (criterion 5).** The second paragraph outlines the aim of the report (looking at the possibility of introducing an alternative treatment) and refers to a systematic review that will (presumably) be discussed. Finally, there is an overview of the contents, reflecting the assignment brief: the report will discuss the history, rationale and evidence – leading to an informed decision about using acupuncture to treat chronic asthma.

---

box 6.2

Example of a good introduction

The following introduction is taken from a student assignment, which asked students to evaluate a complementary therapy:

> Assignment question/brief: Having been employed in a local health clinic, your manager has asked you to write a 2,000 word report outlining your views and specific recommendations about using a complementary therapy. The report should discuss the history, underlying principles and research for the therapy. You should justify your choice of therapy as being relevant to the clinic where you are working.

> **Essay title: A review of acupuncture as an alternative treatment for chronic asthma**

> ### 1. Introduction

> According to the National Asthma Campaign, there are 5.4 million people in the UK currently receiving treatment for asthma and the cost to the NHS is over £996 million per year[1]. In 2007, Killingham's Primary Care Trust had the 4th highest hospital admissions rate for asthma[2] in the whole of the UK, which suggests that the management, treatment and education of asthma are not effective in the Killingham area. New strategies to help reduce strain on emergency departments, respiratory clinics and local GP surgeries need to be brought into play to ensure that asthma sufferers are receiving the treatment they require, when they need it.

> ✓

This introductory paragraph states the scale of the problem, providing general statistics *and* local statistics – making an interesting argument for looking at acupuncture, justifying and contextualising the issue for the assignment.

> This report will focus on the possibility of introducing a complementary and alternative medicine as a treatment option for chronic

(Continued)

(Continued)

asthma at the Killingham Royal Infirmary (KRI) Respiratory Clinic[3]. In 2003, McCarney et al. carried out a systematic review on investigating the effects of acupuncture[20] in treating chronic asthma. This review has recently been updated, sparking new interest in the treatment. The history, rationale and evidence of the alternative therapy will be critically reviewed in this report, leading to an informed consideration of whether acupuncture has a potential role in treating chronic asthma, and essentially in the health care system.

✓

This second paragraph focuses on a particular clinic addressing the assignment question, and provides an overview of contents - history, rationale and evidence 'critically reviewed', as requested in assignment brief.

It is worth noting that this introduction is 200 words in length – which is 10% of the assignment. Given the importance of a clear introduction which summarises the contents of an assignment, I would recommend that an introduction is at least this length. Indeed, my only slight criticism is that the introduction might also have given an indication of what the assignment concludes – is the recommendation in favour or against the use of acupuncture as a treatment for asthma? For example, the writer might have added:

It is concluded, based on this review of the evidence, that acupuncture may have a role to play in the treatment of asthma, but further research is needed in case of possible adverse effects.

Box 6.3 provides an example of a poor introduction – a second-rate version of the one provided in Box 6.2. In comparison, it is short, vague, cursory and tokenistic.

box 6.3

Example of a poor introduction

Essay title: Acupuncture as a treatment for pain

Introduction

This assignment will provide a discussion of the principles and practices of acupuncture. The assignment will provide a brief background to acupuncture, look at the practice, and discuss the evidence from research. Some types of health problems it might be used for, and risks, are also discussed. Finally, the conclusion will end with a discussion of my recommendations about using acupuncture.

× ☹

While this introduction does provide an overview of the contents, it's very tokenistic. Compared to the very good introduction in Box 6.2, this is just a vague regurgitation of the assignment brief. It needed to be longer, more specific and detailed.

Tip 24: Complete the writing of your introduction after you've written your assignment

If the introduction is going to provide an overview of what is in your assignment (the topics, issues and argument), it is better to write it up properly after you've completed the assignment. So it's pointless agonising over it too much before you start. A rough outline should suffice until the assignment is completed.

Tip 25: Write 'a lot about a little' rather than 'a little about a lot'

Chris Mounsey (2002: 30) makes an interesting observation about the transition from school to university:

> An important difference in essay writing between undergraduate level and school … is that at the higher level you are graded more on your ability to make a coherent argument, and less on the amount of information presented. The way to think about it is to remember that in all the essays you have written so far, you have had to say a little about a lot of information. In an undergraduate essay, you need to say a lot about a little bit of information.

In other words, you need to focus. However, this does not mean, for example, providing every minute detail of a research study. Rather, it's about focusing on a few things in depth rather than many things superficially (depth rather than breadth).

Why is this relevant to introductions? Well, because the introduction needs to set the parameters, the scope and the focus of the assignment. In a typical 2,000-word assignment you can only cover so much about a topic, so you have to be selective. If you acknowledge this in your introduction, it shows that you are aware of the broader issues, but that you have set your parameters. As we shall see later, this strategy is also important to avoid covering too much ground (superficially) at the cost of more detailed argument and analysis.

Conclusions

Conclusions are *very* important. Remember, this is the last thing a marker will read before they turn to the marking sheet.

Tip 26: **Provide a good conclusion summarising your answer to the question**

What tutors like

- An ability to sum up
- A concise conclusion that reflects the introduction and the student's own conclusion
- A good conclusion, summarising the answer to the question
- A conclusion that really does conclude what has been presented

A good conclusion should be arrived at: if you've written your assignment well, your conclusion should be obvious, since it should summarise the arguments made throughout the body of the essay.

The study by Townsend et al. (1993), referred to earlier, examined a range of essay-writing guides and arrived at three criteria for an effective conclusion. A good conclusion should:

1. Summarise the main ideas of the essay
2. Provide an answer to the question posed
3. Discuss the broader implications of the topic

Using these criteria, they constructed a conclusion for the essay 'Discuss the role of genetic and environmental factors in IQ scores' and came up with the example provided in Box 6.4.

box 6.4

A model conclusion

This is the 'model' conclusion constructed by Townsend et al. (1993), using key criteria from essay writing guides, for the essay title 'Discuss the role of genetic and environmental factors in IQ scores':

In conclusion, statements such as 'Geniuses are born not made' are too simplistic. The evidence from studies of twins and adopted children demonstrates the importance of both genetic and environmental factors in the development of intelligence. While the genotype may set the upper and lower limits for development, a range of environmental factors determine the extent to which that potential will be realized. Rather than attempting to answer the 'nature vs nurture' question, researchers should investigate ways to enhance the cognitive potential of all individuals.

Notice how this conclusion:

- starts by referring back to the opening quote
- summarises the outcomes from the evidence discussed
- discusses broader implications by making recommendations about further research

In Box 6.5 I have also provided the conclusion from the student assignment discussed earlier, which does a fairly good job of meeting these criteria within the context of a 2,000-word assignment.

box 6.5

Example of a good conclusion

The conclusion below is taken from the student assignment discussed earlier, in which the student evaluated the use of acupuncture for chronic asthma.

Conclusion

In conclusion, the McCarney et al. systematic review has been critically analysed to allow consideration of whether acupuncture would be useful treating asthma at the KRI Respiratory Clinic. The background, rationale and efficacy of the alternative treatment have been reviewed and it has been suggested as a treatment option at the Clinic. Further research is needed into the area along with analysis of the treatment's adverse effects in relation to chronic asthma. Acupuncture may have a role in the health care system as there were some positive findings in the review. Whether these are purely placebo-based may have to be further researched, so more funding will be needed.

This provides a good conclusion to the assignment, with recommendations:

(Continued)

(Continued)

1   It provides a summary - the assignment has critically analysed the evidence (from a systematic review) as well as reviewing the background, rationale and efficacy of the treatment (all as requested in the assignment question and guidelines).

2   It provides an answer to the question posed - based on this review the conclusion says that acupuncture is recommended as a treatment option for the clinic.

3   It also refers to broader implications by identifying limitations of the report and further areas of research - the issue of possible adverse effects and placebo effects, which may require further research or monitoring if acupuncture is used as a treatment in the clinic.

Tip 27: Do not introduce new information in your conclusion

And remember, a conclusion should summarise what has been discussed – it should not introduce new information:

What tutors dislike

•   New information in the conclusion

•   Things talked about in conclusion that were not discussed in the body of the text leaving me to go back to see if I missed it!

Tip 28: Write your conclusion before you start and your introduction after you've finished (eh?)

We already know (Tip 24) that you should complete the writing of your introduction after you've finished your assignment, so you can provide an overview of the contents – what you've actually discussed. By the same token, you might like to formulate your conclusion before you start, remembering that 'clever people work backwards' (Tip 5). To use our analogy of a journey again, it's no good charting the route before the destination has been decided.

General structure and organisation

In the survey of tutors, issues relating to structure came seventh in the list of common problems and fourth on the list of things that impress markers.

Problems relating to structure

Problems included:

- hopping from one theme to another - and back again
- lack of signposting
- lack of headings
- use of appendices

The following tips address each of these issues.

Tip 29: Don't hop about: keep all the information on one issue / theme / topic in one place

One of the main causes of marker distress was essays that lack a logical development and seem to flit back and forth from one theme to the next:

What tutors dislike

- Essays that lack structure and seem to hop from one theme to the next at random; no sense of flow, very little (if any) signposting
- Poor structure, which means going back and forth through pages
- Poor structure, which means that you comment on the absence of detail when the relevant detail appears later on

These last two comments certainly hit a nerve, especially when you've made notes on the script about the need for further details only to find said details turning up later in the essay. The key point here, then, is to keep all the information on one issue, theme or topic together.

Tip 30: Use signposting to summarise and make your essay flow

What tutors like

- Clear signposting of ideas that enables the work to flow in a log-ical manner to a conclusion

- A clear structure, especially when signposted

- Logical structure so the marker is not required to keep going over parts that have already been read in order to keep a grasp of how the parts of the assignment/ essay interrelate

- That the points made clearly link into each other

We've already talked about signposting in the context of introductions, but signposting is also an important strategy throughout the assignment. At certain points/junctures it is useful to provide a brief reflective review of your argu-ment and look towards the next section of the assignment. For example, you might make the transition from one section to another like this:

> Having critically appraised the underlying rationale for acupuncture, we will now examine the evidence from research studies.

> There have been hundreds of studies over the years, but I will be focusing on two recent systematic reviews as the best source of evidence ...

This helps you *and your tutor* to monitor your argument and the points you are making.

Tip 31: Use headings (and subheadings) to structure your work

Personally, I like headings. You know where you are with headings. Literally – as a writer or as a reader/marker – you can see what's where.

What tutors like

- Good use of headings and subheadings

- Use of subtitles – as long as the discussion then matches the subtitle!

Headings and subheadings are useful because they help to structure an assignment into manageable chunks. They can also help to show that you've addressed the relevant areas in the right proportions. In the complementary therapies assignment, for example, students often used the following headings:

- Introduction

- Historical Background

- Rationale of Therapy

- Principles of Practice

- Research Evidence

- Conclusion

These headings are useful to ensure that the relevant issues are covered in the assignment.

However, if you are using headings/subheadings to help structure and organise your assignment, don't overdo it. Too many headings may be disruptive; they should only be used to delineate major sections of a report. So if you end up with 40 headings in your 2,000-word assignment, something is not right.

Tip 32: Check with your tutor about the use of headings

The use of headings may depend on the type of assignment. Strictly speaking, using headings in an essay may not be recommended by some tutors, especially if it's a very short essay, but for research reports or projects they are extremely important and, indeed, essential to ensure that all relevant aspects of the project are clearly reported. Since these are a special case, I've provided a brief outline of the typical sections used in a research report in Chapter 15 (which also includes some common problems).

Note: if your tutor is an essay purist and does not want you to insert headings, you can always write it with headings to help you structure the assignment, and then remove them when you actually submit the assignment. But don't forget to check the flow after you've removed the headings; you may need to add some linking sentences.

Tip 33: Don't use appendices as a dumping ground

Problems with appendices were noted by quite a few tutors and, in fact, came eighth on the list of common problems.

What tutors dislike

- Appendices that are not referred to or discussed in an assignment or have little point for being there

- Putting lots of information in appendices and expecting me to sift through it for the relevant bits

- Poor use (almost any use) of appendices, usually an attempt to gain more words

Appendices are used to provide further information that is relevant but not essential to the main body of a report (if it is essential information, it should be included in the body of the assignment). They are more typically used in reports, such as research proposals, or portfolios of work, to include additional materials that would otherwise clutter up the main body of the text, for example a copy of a questionnaire referred to in the main text, or tables of raw data which, importantly, should have been summarised in the main text. They should not be used as an attempt to gain more words since they are not usually included in the word count of an assignment. If the information is important and necessary to address the assignment question/brief, it should be integrated into the body of the text. Appendices should be treated as additional information which may be consulted by the interested reader.

If you do need to include appendices make sure you refer to them in the text (they should be numbered of course) and also guide the reader through the information. Do not use it as a dumping ground and expect your tutor to sift through it for relevant information. On a practical note, it can sometimes be difficult for the marker to locate the relevant appendix in larger documents (such as dissertations, which may include quite a few appendices), so it's helpful if you can include the page number to help the marker locate it, for example '(see Appendix 10 on p. 79)'.

summary

In this chapter we've seen the crucial importance of:

- providing a good introduction which outlines the content of your assignment (along with five key criteria that could raise your grade)
- concluding your assignment with a summary of what you said and how you've answered the question
- using 'signposting' (in the introduction and throughout the assignment) to help the reader navigate through the assignment

- using headings to structure your assignment
- focusing the scope of your assignment (by writing a lot about a little, rather than a little about a lot)

We've also seen the importance of first impressions – how the 'halo effect' and 'confirmation bias' may influence the marker in subtle ways. There's an interesting phenomenon in psychology which shows that our memory is influenced by what are known as 'primacy' and 'recency' effects (Murdock, 1962; Jones et al., 1968). For example, we tend to remember the first words and the last words in a list more than those in the middle. You might like to think about this when writing your assignment. It would suggest that the introduction and the conclusion are disproportionately prevalent in a tutor's thoughts when it comes to completing the mark sheet. In other words, it's back to making a good first impression and a good last impression.

7

What was the question again?

RTFQ!

Read the Question!

A gentle reminder...

Illustration 7.1

In the survey of tutors, 'failing to answer the question' took top spot as having the most negative impact on the mark. Fairly obvious, you might say, but you'd be surprised how often students fail to answer the question in favour of their own interpretation and preferences – rather like the following advice from Quentin Crisp:

> If you are revising for an exam on geography and the exam could be on any country in the world, study only one country, and know it well. Let's say you choose China. When it comes round to the exam, and the question is, Write 1,000 words on France, you begin your essay, France is nothing like China..., and proceed to write everything you know about China. (Fountain, 1999)

This problem was highlighted in the following comments from the survey. We can see that the main concerns were that students were not answering the question *as set*, drifting off topic and not including the assignment title or paraphrasing it.

What tutors dislike

- Failing to answer the question or task set/writing off topic

- Question not answered – when they start answering the question and by paragraph four they are answering a whole different question which they plucked from the ether somewhere

- Not including the title – or paraphrasing it – missing out the important bits

- Writing an abridged version of the essay question on the front page (and then of course failing to answer the question as set)

What they liked to see, as the comments below illustrate, are students who explicitly address the question, following guidelines and consulting the marking criteria.

What tutors like

Addressing the question

- Addressing the question – and showing they're answering the question

- Addressing the remit of the assignment

Following guidelines

- When the student has managed to follow the guidelines in terms of answering the question

- Having followed closely the assignment guidelines that are provided

- Demonstrating application to learning outcomes, particularly on knowledge and understanding

Consulting the marking criteria

- Reference and thought put into the marking criteria

- Criteria are met or if missed has a good explanation as to the reason why

In this chapter we'll look at each of these issues in turn:

- Addressing the question (and showing that you are addressing the question)

- Following the assignment guidelines/assignment brief (if they exist)

- Checking the learning outcomes and the marking criteria

Tip 34: Include the question at the beginning of the assignment

You should *always* include the assignment question at the start of your work, partly to remind the tutor what the question was – not because they're old and may have forgotten (although this shouldn't be discounted), but in case there was more than one question set, or perhaps a different tutor is marking it, not the tutor who set the assignment. More importantly, though, it should be there to remind *you* of the question you're supposed to be addressing. The absence of the title on an assignment may be a simple oversight, but it is one of those 'this doesn't bode well' moments.

Tip 35: Do not write an abridged version of the question or rephrase it in your own words

For example, here's an essay title I set for a second-year complementary therapies course:

Critically appraise one complementary therapy and its potential role in the health service.

And here are some examples of abridged titles that were produced by students on the cover of their assignments:

- An essay on homeopathy

- Acupuncture

- Assignment: Complementary therapy: Osteopathy

- Osteopathy assignment for complementary therapies

Now, the fact that these students failed to write the question out verbatim did not necessarily mean that they would fail to answer the question, but it doesn't bode well when you see these abridged titles – especially when the most important bits of the question are missing, in this case 'critically appraise' and 'its role in the health service'. It's not an essay 'about' acupuncture or homeopathy; it's an essay which, in order to receive a high mark, needs to critically appraise a complementary therapy in terms of its potential role in the health service.

Tip 36: **Analyse the question**

To 'analyse' means to examine something by breaking it down into simpler elements, and it's what we've just been talking about with regard to answering the complementary therapies question:

> <u>Critically appraise</u> <u>one complementary therapy</u> and its <u>potential role in the health service</u>

Notice that I've underlined three parts:

1. There needs to be critical appraisal

2. This needs to be applied to one complementary therapy

3. And it should focus on its potential role in the health service

This may look a bit nerdy, but the fact that many students fail to answer the question suggests to me that breaking it down into specific elements and underlining key words/phrases of an assignment question is important.

Tip 37: **Define the terms: analyse, discriminate (and problematise)**

An assignment question will often include words and concepts that need to be analysed and defined before you can begin your discussion. In the above example, this would apply to the term 'complementary therapy' – how does it differ from a 'conventional therapy' or an 'alternative therapy'? In thinking about this, you would be embarking on the very important journey of discrimination, showing that you are knowledgeable about the subject and that you are aware of the differences. This would be an important first step in addressing this particular essay question, perhaps providing one or two definitions from key texts (*not* from dictionary.com or wisegeek.com) along with some examples of what are considered to be complementary *and/or* alternative therapies.

Here's another slightly more awkward assignment question to illustrate the point:

> Essay question: 'Good health depends upon social, environmental and economic factors such as deprivation, housing, education and nutrition'. Discuss.

Here again it would be necessary to start by defining the terms used in the question. What is good health? Are we talking about physical health/disease or mental health – or both? Then we need to think about what is meant by 'social, environmental and economic factors'. The question provides some examples but you might think about each in turn:

- Social factors that might affect health: family, relationships, work, leisure, education?

- Environmental factors that affect health: pollution, transport, housing?

- Economic factors: finances, welfare benefits, employment?

Now, obviously you wouldn't want to get too bogged down in this, but it is crucial that you think carefully about the question and the terms used. This would be a necessary first step in scoping your approach to this assignment. Perhaps you might state at the outset that you are focusing on mental health issues rather than physical health. You might even decide to focus on mental health and deprivation. We all know what 'deprivation' is – right? Table 7.1 provides an 'index of deprivation' produced by the sociologist Peter Townsend.

Table 7.1   Townsend deprivation index (adapted from Townsend, 1979)

Criteria for 'deprivation'

1 Not had a holiday away from home in last 12 months
2 Adults only: not had a relative/friend home to eat in last 4 weeks
3 Adults only: not visited friend/relative in the last 4 weeks for a meal
4 Children only (under 15): not had friend to play/for tea in last 4 weeks
5 Children only: not had a party on their last birthday
6 Not going out for entertainment in the last 2 weeks
7 Not having fresh meat at least 4 times a week
8 Not having a cooked meal one day in a fortnight
9 Not having a cooked breakfast most days of the week
10 Not having a house with a refrigerator
11 Where the household does not usually have a Sunday joint
12 Where the household lacks sole use of four key amenities: flush w/c, sink/washbasin, fixed bath/shower, gas/electric cooker

Hopefully, having considered the criteria for 'deprivation' in Table 7.1, you've realised that concepts like this are not 'unproblematic'. When I presented this list to a group of students, their comments were along the following lines:

- Where did the list come from - what's it based on? (A survey of 2,000 households.)

- When was it produced - don't all people these days have a fridge, toilet, etc.? (The 1970s.)

- What if people don't want to go on holiday - even though they can afford to?

- What about vegetarians who don't eat meat?

- What about people from other cultures who don't have a 'Sunday joint' (a phrase which drew a few giggles)?

The point is, then, that your essay question may require some initial ground-work – defining the terms and the scope of your discussion. This may be relatively straightforward for some questions, but for others it might take a little more thought, as this example illustrates. If there's evidence that you've thought about the terms under discussion, this will impress the marker and should help in the construction of your assignment (scope and focus).

Tip 38: What's the point? Refer back to the question (avoid the 'so what?' comment)

It's often a good idea to refer back to the question during your assignment to clearly demonstrate the relevance of what you are talking about and the role it plays in answering the question. For example, in the complementary therapies assignment discussed above ('Critically appraise one complementary therapy...'), the following passage, providing some background about acu-puncture, might be quite interesting, but it would be skimmed over as merely descriptive information at best or, at worst, it might be accompanied by the comment 'so what?' from your tutor:

> Acupuncture has been used in China for over 2,000 years. According to traditional Chinese Medicine, the body has 12 'meridians' (channels through-out the body) through which energy called 'qi' (pronounced 'chee') flows. Ill health and disease occur when there is a disturbance or blockage of this energy along one of the meridians. Needles are inserted at particular 'acu-puncture points' on the meridians to stimulate the flow of 'qi' in order to address imbalances or blockages in energy, thereby restoring health.

This is a nice summary of how acupuncture is supposed to work according to traditional theories, but 'so what?' What role does this have to play in address-ing the question? However, if this passage is 'framed', with explicit reference to how this information is addressing the question, it takes on a whole new significance and relevance.

> In order to decide if acupuncture has a role to play in the health service it is important to consider its historical origins and underlying rationale. This will give us some insight into the plausibility of the treatment.
>
> Acupuncture has been used in China for over 2,000 years. According to traditional Chinese Medicine, the body has 12 'meridians' (channels through-out the body) through which energy called 'qi' (pronounced 'chee') flows. Ill health and disease occur when there is a disturbance or blockage of this energy along one of the meridians. Needles are inserted at particular 'acu-puncture points' on the meridians to stimulate the flow of 'qi' in order to address imbalances or blockages in energy, thereby restoring health.
>
> These traditional beliefs are not supported by our current physiological knowl-edge of the human body: there has been no evidence to confirm the existence of an energy called 'qi', or meridians. Therefore, on the basis of the under-lying principles, acupuncture could not be recommended. However, research

has suggested that the insertion of acupuncture needles releases endorphins, which act to reduce pain. It is to this research evidence that we now turn. ...

By 'framing' the passage in this way, the relevance of this descriptive information in terms of answering the question becomes explicitly apparent; it has turned the passage into an argument. As we shall see in the next chapter, this is crucial for a good assignment.

Tip 39: Follow the assignment guidelines/brief for answering the question

Your assignment may be accompanied by some additional guidelines in the form of an assignment brief outlining what is expected in terms of the topics/issues you should be covering (and perhaps even the structure of the assignment). If it does, pay close attention to this because it will provide you with some important clues about what your tutor is expecting in the assignment. I've reproduced the assignment question and brief from the complementary therapies assignment below for illustration:

Assignment question

Having graduated in medicine or another health profession, you have become gainfully employed in a local health clinic. The manager of the clinic is interested to know more about complementary and alternative therapies due to their growing popularity amongst patients and so asks you to write a 2,000 word report outlining your views and specific recommendations for possible referrals of patients to complementary therapists.

Assignment brief

Your assignment should show that you have developed a critical understanding of the topic which should require reference to the history and underlying principles of complementary and alternative medicine (CAM) and the research evidence. Your discussion of these issues should not be purely descriptive but should involve analysis and critical appraisal of CAM with reference to the best evidence for your conclusions.

You should justify your choice of content as being relevant to the clinic where you are hypothetically working (e.g. prevalence of health problems), and provide a succinct overview of the content and argument in a brief introduction/abstract to the report. The conclusion should summarise the content and your argument.

Note: You cannot cover all complementary therapies in your report; you should focus on just one or two that you think are most relevant.

I've extracted the key components from this assignment brief and listed them below:

1. Provide a succinct overview of the content and argument in a brief introduction/abstract to the report.

2. Justify your choice of content as being relevant to the clinic where you are hypothetically working (e.g. prevalence of health problems).

3. Focus on just one or two therapies that you think are most relevant.

4. Discuss the history and underlying principles of your therapy.

5. Discuss the best research evidence for your conclusions.

6. Provide a conclusion summarising the content and your argument.

Assignment briefs are used to highlight key issues that should be discussed, so study them carefully if you want to 'tick all the boxes' and receive a high mark. This is why it's a good idea to structure your assignment using headings – to ensure that all parts of the assignment are covered (see Tip 31). You can always remove the headings once you've completed the assignment if your tutor has advised against them (not forgetting to add a few linking sentences where the headings have been removed).

It's also important to note that if the assignment requires you to do things in a particular order (e.g. a series of exercises) or follow a particular report structure – stick to it. If it's been specified in the guidelines, there's probably a good reason for it. For example, your tutor may be assigning marks for discrete exercises; if you diverge from the guidelines – the prescribed structure – you might be making it difficult for the tutor to mark your work.

Tip 40: Check the learning outcomes

If your module has some 'learning outcomes', and it probably should do these days, make sure you know what they are. Your assignment, and your mark, will ultimately be judged against them. They should be available in the course/module handbook (and/or the course/module descriptor).

Learning outcomes will vary in scope and detail, but they should be designed to give you a clear, explicit idea of what you should be demonstrating in your assignment. For example, the module about complementary and alternative medicine includes the following 'learning outcomes':

On successful completion of this module you will be able to:

Demonstrate understanding of the <u>historical origins</u>, <u>rationale</u>, <u>practice</u> and <u>evidence base</u> for a complementary therapy.

Notice that there are four criteria here to be addressed if you want to achieve a high mark in the assignment, and they should *all* be addressed, although the extent to which each is addressed in the assignment will depend upon their particular relevance to the topic and the approach taken in answering the question.

Some academics are critical of the 'learning outcomes approach' to teaching. The concern is that they can be too prescriptive, stifling a more creative, personal voyage of discovery (Hussey and Smith, 2010). On the positive side, though, they do help to make clear what's expected in assignments, thereby helping to address a common complaint from students – that they don't know what the tutor really wants.

Tip 41: Consult the marking criteria

After the tutor has read your assignment and made some comments/notes, they will then refer to the marking criteria/assessment sheet. Although these vary in structure and emphasis, and the weight accorded to each criterion, they usually cover the following areas:

- **Written expression.** Was it difficult to read, with many spelling mistakes and grammatical errors? Or was it well written, with clarity of expression?

- **Structure and presentation.** Was it poorly structured and presented, making it difficult to follow, or was it well structured, clearly guiding the reader through the issues? (Note my use of 'reader' rather than 'tutor' – we'll come to the issue of the audience you should be writing for later.)

- **Understanding of the issues.** Did it demonstrate understanding of the issues and coverage of the learning outcomes for the course? (As noted above, the learning outcomes should be listed in the module descriptor.) Was there perceptive discussion of the issues, or was it all quite superficial ('a little about a lot' rather than 'a lot about a little')?

- **Reading.** Did it refer to the relevant literature, or were there serious omissions? Were a variety of sources used? (While it's good to find your own references, the absence of key references referred to in lectures can be a major oversight.)

- **Evaluation, analysis and critical thought.** Was there evaluation and critical appraisal of the issues, or was it mainly descriptive?

- **Conclusions.** Were conclusions made and presented, or was it all left up in the air?

- **Referencing.** Were the references all present and in the correct format, or were some missing and/or not properly presented?

Having read the assignment, your tutor will go through these criteria one by one and put a tick by the most appropriate grade, after which they will review where the ticks are and arrive at the mark. Generally speaking, it's as simple as that. It's not a mystical process, and in some cases students are invited to go through this process themselves, by completing a self-assessment form reflecting on how they've addressed the criteria along with a suggested grade. Although tutors and students may differ in their assessment of the work (widely!), this is a useful exercise for any student who wishes to check that their assignment meets the relevant criteria. However, it depends what you write on the self-assessment form. As one of the tutors in the survey pointed out, writing a list of the things you know you didn't do can be annoying – as the following (real) example illustrates:

> ## Self-assessment form (extract)
>
> 'I could have met more key issues'
>
> 'I could have discussed more research'
>
> 'I could have referenced better'

Well, why didn't you, then?

It's also interesting to note that, in my own experience at least, students who have produced a good piece of work tend to underestimate the mark, whereas those who have produced a poor assignment tend to overestimate the mark, which puts me in mind of an article in the *Journal of Personality & Social Psychology* entitled: 'Unskilled and unaware of it: How difficulties in recognising one's own incompetence lead to inflated self-assessments' (Kruger and Dunning, 1999).

Tip 42: Make the transition from being 'unconsciously incompetent' to 'unconsciously competent'

There is an interesting model of learning that's relevant here (developed by Noel Burch at Gordon Training International in the 1970s) which proposes that we move through four stages of competence:

Unconscious incompetence: unaware that you don't know something.

Conscious incompetence: aware that you are incompetent at something.

Conscious competence: competent but have to consciously think about it.

Unconscious competence: competent/skilled and it now comes naturally.

If we apply this to writing assignments, it might look something like Table 7.2.

Table 7.2 Four stages of competence

Stage	Relevance to writing assignments
Unconscious incompetence	Writing essays and assignments is easy. I just need to describe and report what others have written.
Conscious incompetence	I've just received my mark and feedback. Apparently, it's important to analyse and critique what I read, but I'm not sure what this is and how to do it.
Conscious competence	I'm aware about analysis now and I always try to remember to add some critical comments.
Unconscious competence	As soon as I looked at that theory/model/statistic, I thought 'how do they know this?', 'who says so?', 'what's the evidence?'

Hopefully these tips, and particularly those in the next chapter, will transform you into an 'unconsciously competent' student.

summary

Why do some students fail to answer the question? Because it's usually easier not to answer the question – it's much easier to just report a lot of things you've found out about a topic and/or what you're interested in (or, as sometimes happens, reproduce lots of material from a previous assignment which has a vague relevance). This was highlighted in the quote from Quentin Crisp at the beginning of the chapter, and is illustrated in the following comments from tutors cited in Norton et al. (2009: 49–50):

> They look at the question and start off with an introduction and say this is what I'm going to answer, but then they wander off and talk about something entirely different.

> People are more likely to fail or do badly if they just write everything they know about a topic and don't focus on the question. It's just that to me a 2:1 answers the question, but a 2:2 talks about the topic without necessarily answering the question.

> Students struggle with addressing the question sometimes because, whether it's in coursework or exams, they want to tell you what they know. If they feel confident with the bit that they know about, so long as it has some vague relationship to what you've asked, then they're going to tell you all about it.

In the next chapter we'll see that this desire to convey all that you know about a topic is a big mistake, and is actually a common misconception among students.

8

Critical analysis, perspective and argument

If you can't say anything nice, don't say anything at all.

(Old English proverb)

Good advice for social occasions, perhaps, but potentially disastrous for your assignments.

In this chapter we'll be discussing the importance of adopting a critical perspective, developing an argument, and making a case for the position you have decided to adopt. To help you appreciate the significance of this when writing your assignments, we'll be looking at:

- a model of learning and teaching that probably forms the basis for how your course is taught and how your assignments are assessed
- some questions you might ask when presented with a theory, a model, or the findings from a research study
- a crucial difference between what you think is important when writing your assignments and what tutors think is important when marking your assignments
- the importance of adopting a perspective on the issues you are discussing (and making a case for your position)

You'll also learn that there are no 'right' answers, and that you should trust no one.

Tip 43: **Stop describing, start critiquing**

One of the most significant outcomes from the survey is that it highlights the importance of critical thinking and argument as the feature that tutors value highest when marking assignments. The message is that you need to step up a gear: from simply describing and reporting to being analytical, critical and evaluative. In this respect, there's something you should know about. It's called Bloom's taxonomy (Figure 8.1) and it probably forms the basis for how your course is taught and assessed.

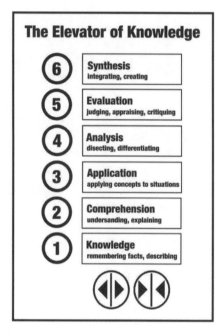

Figure 8.1 Illustration of Bloom's taxonomy of educational objectives

Bloom's taxonomy (Bloom et al., 1956) outlines six levels of thinking, from the simple to the complex. Pay particular attention to what lies at the bottom in Figure 8.1: description, recalling facts, and simply reporting what others have said. If you want high marks, particularly as you progress through the years at university, you will need to climb this ladder by applying, analysing and critically evaluating concepts.

So you start by building up your knowledge about a concept, theory, model, etc. until you are able to understand it, describe it, give examples and then apply it, but then you progress beyond this level of understanding (merely knowing about and accepting something because it's in a book or a manual) to a more critical, analytical perspective.

Generally speaking, then, description won't get you many marks; it certainly won't get you high marks. So, if the question asks you to 'analyse', 'critically appraise' or 'evaluate' and you spend most of the essay describing things, reporting lots of facts and figures and covering as much ground as possible, you're heading for disappointment. This emphasis on critical analysis rather than description is highlighted in the comments from the survey of tutors:

What tutors dislike

- Description rather than analysis (particularly from second year upwards)

- Presenting lots of bullet points instead of discussion

- Long bits of description which could be condensed into a sentence or two

- Not providing some sort of critique of, or reflection on, the work they've read (i.e. assuming because it's in print it must be 'right')

What tutors like

- Students who attempt to look critically at models/theories

- Analysis of reading rather than description

- Concise critical appraisal (with citations in support, where appropriate)

- Ability to see more than one side of an argument

- Being aware that just because something is in print it doesn't make it a for-all-time, concrete, unassailable fact!

- A good mixture of discussion and argument

- Comparison of sources and analysis

- Critical comment on the literature (author A takes this view in contrast to author B – what they both fail to account for fully is...; or an alternative interpretation can be offered by...; or this does not account for the problematic nature of [this concept], etc.)

Tip 44: When presented with a theory, a model, or the findings from a research study, there are certain questions you should ask

If you are going to adopt a more critical perspective, it's useful to have some questions at the ready to get you started (Neville, 2009a; G. Taylor, 2009). I've listed a few below along with some examples of how they might be applied.

Where does the theory/model/statistic come from? Who says? How do they know? What's the evidence? What's the sample?

Did you know, for example, that women talk more than men? Of course you did: an average 20,000 words per day compared to 7,000 for men. When these statistics were featured in *The Female Brain*, a bestselling book by Louann Brizendine

(2006), they were circulated throughout the media (e.g. 'Women talk three times as much as men, says study' was the headline in the *Daily Mail* newspaper; Macrae, 28 November 2006). However, on closer inspection it was discovered that these figures were derived from a self-help book and other second-hand sources – not research – and they were removed from a later edition of the book (Lilienfeld et al., 2010). A more reliable primary source based on a study by Mehl et al. (2007), reported in the journal *Science*, found that men and women both use around 16,000 words per day, though with 'very large individual differences'.

Does it make sense based on your own experience?

Your own experience may lead you to question the conclusions from the Mehl et al. (2007) study. There were, after all, 'very large individual differences', and the study was based on a particular sample: 396 university students (210 were female).

Does it apply across different contexts and cultures?

We should also question whether these results apply across different contexts and cultures since the study was limited to a sample of university students from the USA.

Does it apply in the real world?

When Newstead and Dennis (1994) asked 14 experienced examiners to mark six essays some of the marks were so inconsistent that they ranged from a 2:2 to a first – for the same essay. Does this mean that the mark you are awarded for your assignment depends to a large extent on the tutor who is marking it? Not necessarily, because this was an experiment rather than real-life marking with real consequences for the student. Furthermore, the marking was conducted by tutors not involved on the course, it was a 'rather abstract and obscure topic that examiners might have great difficulty in marking' (Newstead, 2002: 73), and they weren't using marking schemes with clear criteria. In research terms, this is known as lacking 'ecological validity', because the study didn't really reflect the real-life situation.

Is it plausible?

The problem with research is that it can be contradictory. Think about health advice: one minute we are advised to eat fewer eggs and the next minute we are told we can eat as many as we like (within reason of course). In my own area of interest, complementary and alternative therapies, there have been decades of research providing conflicting evidence on whether treatments like homeopathy or acupuncture work or not. While it's important to be selective about the evidence you choose to believe (the more robust studies), it's also important to look at the *plausibility* of the treatments: what's the rationale – the underlying mechanism of action? Is it plausible that acupuncture works because it claims to release a mysterious 'energy' called 'qi' through equally mysterious channels referred to as meridians? At this point you might want to consider carefully the underlying rationale for a particular therapy. We would apply the same criteria to pseudosciences like astrology.

Are there exceptions which challenge the theory/model?

Most students in the social sciences will at one time or another come across Abraham Maslow's (1987) famous model outlining the 'hierarchy of human

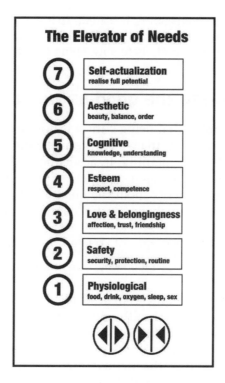

Figure 8.2   Illustration of Maslow's hierarchy of human needs

needs'. I've represented it as an 'elevator of needs' in Figure 8.2. The model has been used to account for why most people are never satisfied: having satisfied one set of needs, our priorities move on to the next. For example, once you've achieved safety and security (job, house, etc.), you might then start to focus on 'love and belongingness' (personal and social relationships); and once that's sorted out, you might start to think about your esteem needs (e.g. promotion at work); and so on. The problem is, of course, that there are many exceptions. For example, many people in affluent countries are satisfied with a house, car, family, etc., and don't crave a higher level of 'self-actualisation' epitomised by the famous few upon which Maslow's concept of 'self-actualisation' was based (e.g. Albert Einstein, Abraham Lincoln). They may be happy with their lot. Another problem is the idea that we have to satisfy needs at one level before moving on to the next. For example, must we satisfy the more basic physiological needs before dealing with the higher needs? (Dear Tutor, I won't be attending your lecture today because I have some needs lower down the hierarchy that I have to satisfy...).

There is an important issue to be aware of here: beware of simplified secondary accounts of a theory. For example, in many textbooks Maslow's hierarchy is criticised for stating that we must satisfy the lower needs before moving up to the higher needs. But Maslow didn't actually say this in such simplistic terms. He took a more realistic approach, pointing out that we move up the hierarchy when lower levels are partially satisfied. New motivations *emerge* as lower needs are becoming fulfilled. He was also well aware of exceptions (e.g. the starving artist who forgoes the more basic needs in favour of aesthetic needs).

This illustrates an important point: be careful that you don't simplify or misinterpret the theory/model. This highlights the importance of comparing a few sources of information and, preferably, going back to the original source.

Tip 45: Appreciate the good as well as the bad

It's important to remember that being critical is not just about being negative. Rather, it's about demonstrating that you appreciate the *pros and cons* – discerning the good and the bad – of something. In academic studies this usually means evaluating a theory, model, research study, etc., but in real life we do it all the time when we make judgements about the quality of a movie, music, fashion, cars, etc. In assignments, though, you just need to be a bit more rigorous:

- What's good about it (and why; with references to support your case)
- What's problematic about it (and why; with references...)

Critically appraising research articles in academic journals is a common assignment topic for students in the health and social sciences. It requires them to appraise the various parts of an article, including the title (is it clear and informative?), the abstract (is it a good summary of the article, providing details about the sample, methods, results?), the methodology (was it appropriate to the aims of the study? Was it clearly explained? Was it well designed?), and so on. It's supposed to be a detailed critical examination of the research, but sometimes this isn't quite achieved, as the following extract from one assignment illustrates:

> **Critically appraising a research article (extract from student assignment)**
>
> The title is easy to read as it has big font and it's bold so it stands out … The abstract is not as clear to read from as it has small font which makes it difficult to read because the words are so close together … The good thing about the abstract is that it's placed in the middle so therefore it differentiates itself from the rest of the literature…

There are lots of books (and many websites) providing guidelines to help you critically appraise the quality and reliability of research studies. In the health sciences, for example, Trisha Greenhalgh's (2006) book, *How to Read a Paper*, is a classic text providing guidance on critically appraising a range of research designs (e.g. randomised controlled trials, systematic reviews, qualitative research).

Tip 46: You think it's all about content and coverage, but tutors value argument and understanding

Studies have highlighted a 'mismatch' between what students and tutors think is most important when writing essays (Norton, 1990; Defeyter and

McPartlin, 2007). While both students and tutors agree that the top rank goes to 'answering the question', a mismatch appears between the importance of content and argument:

- Students rank content and coverage of relevant information higher than argument
- Tutors rank argument and understanding higher than content

Another way of putting this is that tutors place greater emphasis on the importance of a deep approach – displaying *understanding* – whereas students tend to focus on a surface approach – covering lots of information. (Remember Tip 25: you should be writing 'a lot about a little, rather than a little about a lot'.)

Tip 47: Try using the 'therefore test' to check for arguments

If you're not totally clear about what an argument is, and whether your assignment includes any, there's a simple test you can use: see if you can insert the word 'therefore' at the end of a series of statements. Here's a simple example from Richard van de Lagemaat (2007: 10) which illustrates the difference between (1) merely listing a series of unsubstantiated statements and (2) constructing an argument:

1. Astrology is the belief that the position of the stars at the time of your birth affects your destiny. There are ten times more astrologers than astronomers in the United States. Despite its popularity, astrology cannot be classified as a science.

2. One of the hallmarks of a genuine science is that it makes testable predictions. Admittedly, astrologers do make predictions, but they are so vague that they cannot be verified or falsified. So, unlike astronomy, astrology cannot be classified as a science.

Whereas (1) lists a series of unrelated statements, (2) constructs an argument – and we could use 'therefore' to replace 'so' before the final sentence. (Other words like 'so', 'consequently', 'thus', and 'hence' may also be used to indicate the conclusion to an argument.) Out of interest, I decided to go through the excellent student assignment that I referred to in Chapter 6 to see if I could use the 'therefore' test to highlight arguments in the text, and I was pleased to find two opportunities in the opening paragraph of the introduction:

Introduction

According to the National Asthma Campaign, there are 5.4 million people in the UK currently receiving treatment for asthma and the cost to the NHS is over £996 million per year. In 2007, Killingham's Primary Care Trust had the 4th highest hospital admissions rate for asthma in the whole of the UK, which suggests [**therefore**] that the management, treatment and education of asthma is not effective in the Killingham area. [**Therefore**] New strategies to help reduce strain on emergency departments, respiratory clinics and local

GP surgeries need to be brought into play to ensure that asthma sufferers are receiving the treatment they require, when they need it.

Here we can see that the 'therefore test' makes the underlying argument in this introductory passage explicit. If we break it down into premises (statements which lead to a claim), it looks like this:

- Premise 1: Asthma affects millions of people in the UK

- Premise 2: Treatments for asthma costs millions each year

- Premise 3: Killingham Care Trust has one of the highest hospital admission rates in the UK

- Conclusion: Therefore new strategies to treat asthma might be considered: the argument provides a justification for examining the use of acupuncture as an alternative or complementary treatment for asthma

It is this logical reasoning, made explicit by the 'therefore' test, which makes this introduction so effective.

Here's one more illustration of an argument from this excellent assignment:

The review [of research studies] drew limited conclusions regarding the effectiveness of acupuncture in treating asthma. Out of all the trials, only two of them reported the participants to have an improvement in overall well-being and this could not be distinguished between needle or sham acupuncture. Patients who received the acupuncture or believed they were having acupuncture (a placebo) did improve in general health, but not specifically in their asthma symptoms. [**Therefore**] This suggests the placebo effect of acupuncture may play a part in the therapeutic role of the treatment.

If we turn the main argument here into premise and conclusion, it might look like this:

- Premise: Patients who received real acupuncture showed some improvement in general health, but so did those who received sham acupuncture

- Conclusion: This suggests [therefore] that the placebo effect plays a part in the therapeutic role of the treatment

But did you also notice another (related) argument in this passage? Sometimes the conclusion is stated prior to the premise, so if we reverse the first two sentences this reveals another premise and conclusion:

- Premise: Only two of the trials in the review of research studies reported an improvement in well-being

- Conclusion: [Therefore] There is limited evidence regarding the effectiveness of acupuncture in treating asthma

I would suggest (therefore) that this might be a useful test to apply in your assignments to see if they contain any arguments. Though it's important to note, of course, that some arguments are better than others:

> There is a strong correlation between ice-cream sales and crime rates: as ice-cream sales rise, so does the crime rate. Therefore ice-cream causes crime ...

Incidentally, and perhaps unsurprisingly, since writing this book I've witnessed many assignments that are superficially peppered with the word 'therefore'. Remember that the extracts in the excellent complementary therapies assignment that I used to illustrate the presence of arguments didn't actually include the word 'therefore' – I inserted it to make the argument explicit. The point I'm making is: don't overdo it. A student who is comfortable arguing doesn't make it look like a special effort (or a cheap trick). Argument should be implicit in your discussion of the topic, not something that's superficially tagged on at the end of paragraphs with sentences beginning with 'Therefore'.

Tip 48: What do you think? Adopt a perspective - have a point of view

What tutors like

- Balanced argument but own opinion included within the arguments

- Ability to see more than one side of an argument

- The student's own conclusion

- A student not afraid to express an opinion (where relevant)

- A presence of voice - a sense that the author has a 'political' stance, or indeed conviction. The better essays are usually written by those students.

In the study by Defeyter and McPartlin (2007) referred to above, it was also noted that some students felt they shouldn't be presenting a particular view. Rather they should be presenting a balanced evaluation. Well, this is partly true – you should consider different perspectives, both sides of the argument, but as we saw in Chapter 4 (Tips 4 and 5), you should come to some position yourself before you start writing the assignment. What do you think? What will you be ultimately arguing for?

Tip 49: How to make the jump from a B to an A: act like you're a lawyer making a case

I have just spent a couple of hours comparing a batch of assignments which were awarded a B with those that were awarded an A. What was the difference?

Well, while the Bs were generally well written, structured and presented, covered all the key issues and included key references, they didn't make a clear and focused case. Most of the relevant information was there – it just wasn't organised, structured and focused like a first-class essay. This is usually apparent from the start, with a good introduction presaging a clear and focused argument – and everything in the assignment, every section, every paragraph is a building block towards a clear conclusion.

In a good essay you should take a position, take 'a line' on the subject matter, and argue for one or other position – as if you're a lawyer making a case. This will help you to structure the essay, for example, by presenting the case against your argument first, but then presenting the (better) case for your argument afterwards. So any information you are discussing is only relevant to the extent that you are using it to support your case – your argument.

A word of warning, however. I have seen students reduced to a crumbling bag of nerves because they've been told they must include more critical analysis in their assignments. Their ability to write a clear and simple descriptive account goes to pieces in their quest to embark on deep, impenetrable critical discussion. It's about finding a balance: yes, you do need to adopt a critical perspective, but this will include descriptive writing to provide essential background information so that the writing makes sense to the reader.

Tip 50: Support your argument with evidence

Now obviously you'll need to support your arguments with evidence – the best and most reliable and robust evidence – but you already knew that from Chapter 5.

What tutors like

- Statements substantiated
- Backing up of ideas
- Use of good evidence to support assertions, including research findings
- Use and critique of appropriate reference resources that demonstrate a thorough literature search
- Reading widely and using the literature to develop a critical argument
- Critical debate supported with appropriate literature

So when you're advised to say what you think, this doesn't mean, well, just saying what you think – off the top of your head, as it were. It needs to be backed up with evidence or other support.

Tip 51: Illustrate and apply ideas to specific contexts

The survey also highlighted the importance of 'illustrating and applying ideas to specific contexts', grounding the discussion in actual examples, rather than remaining vague about the issues under discussion. In the ranking of themes, this actually came third in the list of what most impresses tutors.

What tutors like

- Relating discussion to actual examples

- Linking theory and practice through the explicit use of examples

- Linking literature to practice

- Reflections on practice that indicate taking the assignment seriously

- Using a case study/example to illustrate their comments/analysis

- Application of the reading and student learning to the context they are discussing/analysing

For example, if you're doing an assignment on some psychological issue, let's say positive and negative reinforcement of behaviour, don't just focus on the experimental studies, relate it to real life – gambling, punishment, learning. How does it work in the real world? So if the theories say 'this' and the research says 'that', think: how does this apply to the real world?

The student assignment that I have been discussing did a very good job of illustrating and applying ideas in the 'real world', particularly in the recommendations section where the *practicalities* of introducing acupuncture as a treatment for asthma are discussed. I've extracted the key passage for illustration in Box 8.1.

box 8.1

Applying the results of research to the real world

The following extract from an example assignment critically reflects on the systematic review of research examining the use of acupuncture for asthma. It highlights the difference between research and practice, and the extent to which results are generalisable and apply in real life (actual practice).

(Continued)

(Continued)

This systematic review has several limitations. Acupuncture trials are highly complex to carry out simply due to the variation in methods. For example, the review did not specifically list the type of needle, needle depth, duration and location of needle insertion for each study, introducing potential bias. This review describes the positive outcome measures of acupuncture but does not mention any adverse effects. This does not give a fair representation of acupuncture as a whole. Another limitation is that it focuses only on mild to moderate asthma, so the findings cannot be generalised for all classifications. Finally, the accuracy of acupuncture used in the trials compared to actual acupuncture practice could be questionable. Acupuncture often comes in a complementary and alternative medicine 'package' which involves lifestyle changes and/or herbal medicines to promote physical - as well as emotional - well-being and is tailored to each person individually. This would not have been achieved in the clinical trials.

Tip 52: There are no 'right' answers - only positions you can adopt and cases you can make

It's often the case that the more you think about an issue, the more difficult it is to provide a simple, straightforward answer. So if you think you have a simple answer to an assignment question, beware. It probably means you've not looked into it deeply enough. As the saying goes: 'The more you know, the less you know.'

When William Perry (1968) studied the intellectual development of students at Harvard University, he discovered a similar progression from certainty to uncertainty. He identified three main stages or 'positions', as he referred to them:

Position 1: Student's view of knowledge is dualistic: there's 'right' and 'wrong', and 'good' and 'bad'. Knowledge consists of objective facts, and authority figures (tutors) and textbooks provide the answers. All you need to do is listen out for the right answers and reproduce them in assignments.

Position 2: Student realises that there is more than one viewpoint - there is diversity of opinion - but the right answers are out there if we can find them. From this perspective, the lecture is like a guessing game in which the student has to figure out which theory is correct but discover the answer themselves.

Position 3: Student sees all knowledge and values as contextual and relative: some solutions are better than others depending on the context - we have to assess and choose. There are no 'right' answers, only positions you can adopt and cases you can make (with supporting evidence and arguments).

Remember that we were talking about 'cue-seekers' in Chapter 3? Well, the researchers, Miller and Partlett (1974), suggest that the cue-seekers (most of whom got a first) have reached this final stage: they are aware that, for many topics, particularly in the social sciences and humanities, there are no 'right' answers – only 'positions' you can adopt and cases you can make (with pros and cons), that are supported by argument and evidence. Think about it.

This sentiment is reflected in a statement by the Higher Education Council of Australia:

> Perhaps the most important 'generic' skill that a graduate can possess is the ability to recognise that knowledge is provisional, and that no answer is final, and that there is always a potential for a better way of doing things. (Cited in Naylor, 2007: 87)

Tip 53: Dare to know

This is the motto of the Enlightenment, a period in the eighteenth century when philosophers questioned the received ideas derived from authorities, traditions and faith. For the philosopher Immanuel Kant (1724–1804), it was about having the courage to use your own understanding; for the philosopher Diderot (1713–1784), it was about questioning everything: 'All things must be examined, debated, investigated without exception and without regard for anyone's feelings ... We must ride roughshod over all ancient puerilities, overturn the barriers that reason never erected' (Diderot, *Encyclopédie*, 1775, cited in Smith, 1998).

This is the attitude you should adopt when you're writing your assignments. The Royal Society, which is the world's oldest scientific academy (founded in 1660) bears a similar motto, *Nullius in verba* – roughly translated as 'Take nobody's word for it' (where's the evidence?).

Tip 54: Trust no one

This is a more contemporary take on the Enlightenment motto, which recognises the fact that, human nature being what it is, people tend to operate with their own interests at heart, and this can lead to all kinds of bias. For example, studies have shown that research funded by pharmaceutical companies is four times more likely to give results that are favourable to the companies than independent studies (Bausell, 2007; Goldacre, 2009). Box 8.2 provides another example of how bias can subtly influence the results of research, illustrating the point that you should trust no one – not even yourself.

box 8.2

Does water remember? (Or 'the devil is in the detail')

In 1988 a paper appeared in the highly prestigious journal *Nature* claiming that an allergen triggered a chemical reaction in cells even after it had been diluted to such an extent that it had long since ceased to contain a single molecule of the original ingredient (after the fifteenth

(Continued)

(Continued)

dilution it would be essentially just water, but they used 120 successive dilutions). One explanation proposed by the director of the research, Jacques Benveniste, was that the water may have retained a memory of the original ingredient. As such, the experiment would provide support for homeopathy, one of the key principles of which is that remedies (mainly herbal) become more powerful the more they are diluted.

Since this was such a remarkable finding, contradicting the laws of physics, *Nature* agreed to publish the paper (Davenas et al., 1988), but with the proviso that they could visit the laboratory to observe how the experiments were being conducted. After observing several repeated experiments, the investigators became concerned that the people recording the changes in the cells knew which ones were being treated with the highly diluted allergen: judging whether a change had occurred was quite subjective and therefore prone to interpretation and bias. So they asked them to repeat the experiment but this time they were 'blinded' to ensure there could be no bias in their observations of changes in the cells: this time there was no effect.

One of the investigators from *Nature* was very relieved: James Randi, a well-known sceptic and magician had staked $1 million on the outcome of the experiment – or any experiment which contradicts the laws of science, including the existence of psychic, supernatural, or paranormal phenomena. The money has been available since 1964 and is still there, unclaimed, to this day (despite over 1000 attempts, and a few famous refusals to accept the challenge).

This shows the importance of 'blinding' in order to avoid unconscious (or deliberate) bias in interpreting data. It also, however, raises some other issues of potential bias. The research was initiated by a young homeopathic doctor, Bernard Poitevin, and the experiments were largely conducted by Elisabeth Davenas who also believed in homeopathy. The laboratory was part funded by a French homeopathic company – the Laboratories Homéopathiques de France.

The investigation by the team from *Nature* was filmed for a BBC *Horizon* programme (26 November 2002). Further details can be found at www.bbc.co.uk/science/horizon/2002/homeopathy.shtml (accessed March 2016).

Tip 55: Ask the question, 'Whose interests are being served here?' (follow the money)

Jeremy Paxman, the presenter of BBC's *Newsnight* for over 20 years, famously said of his approach to interviewing that he starts by asking himself the question, 'Why is this lying bastard lying to me?' Perhaps it's not appropriate for every interview, but when it comes to politicians and people with a vested interest, Paxman advocates a degree of scepticism, asking yourself, 'why are they saying this?' and 'is it likely to be true?' (Wells, 2005).

Continuing on the theme of bias, then, these are important questions to pose when a particular viewpoint may be being promoted. As the example below illustrates, there may be a degree of self-interest, especially where money is involved:

New research claims ten squares of dark chocolate a day for two weeks can cure stress … 'The study shows that a daily consumption of 40 grams over two weeks can modify the metabolism', said Nestlé researcher Sunil Kochhar. (*Metro* newspaper, 13 November 2009)

If you want more details about how self-interest, money and the media can bias the results of research, there are a number of books and internet sources to get your critical juices flowing and develop your 'critical consciousness'. For example, Ben Goldacre has written extensively on these issues in two books (*Bad Science*, 2008, and *Bad Pharma*, 2012) and has a website at http://www.bad science.net/about-dr-ben-goldacre/. On the subject of mental health, James Davies exposes the interests of pharmaceutical companies in his book *Cracked: Why Psychiatry Is Doing More Harm Than Good* (2013). And for a more general exposé on self-interest, politicians and the media, Owen Jones's book *The Establishment: And How They Get Away With It* (2014) examines the extent to which self-interest, power and corruption may be ruling our society, and our lives.

Being critical: Strategies to detect bullshit

In this final part of the chapter I've highlighted three useful strategies for the detection of dubious claims. I've also included a few websites devoted to critical thinking and sceptical inquiry for those of you who don't like being duped.

He used to be happy, but since going to university he never stops moaning...

Illustration 8.1

Tip 56: Apply Occam's razor

Yorkshireman wakes up from a coma speaking fluent Japanese – despite never having been to Japan!

I once overheard a conversation in which this newspaper story (or something similar) was recounted with bewildering interest: a man who'd received a bang on the head fell unconscious, and woke up speaking a different language. In the ensuing discussion it was argued that memories must have been revived from a past life or that there must have been some genes containing Japanese language, handed down from past generations, which had suddenly been released after the bang on the head. Well, that's two possible explanations, but in such circumstances we might do well to apply Occam's razor, which recommends that when two or more theories are competing to explain a phenomenon we should choose the simplest – or the one that makes the fewest assumptions.

So, returning to our proposed explanations for the mysterious case of waking up speaking a foreign language, the assumptions include:

1. We have past lives.
2. We retain memories and skills (like language) from these past lives that can suddenly spring into action.
3. Memories can be passed down through generations, through genes, which contain a whole language.
4. A bang on the head, for some reason, can ignite these memories.

Alternatively, we might opt for the slightly more prosaic and simpler explanation that it's a largely fabricated report by a newspaper based on a grain of truth (he did wake up speaking gibberish which sounded a bit like Japanese), noting the familiar newspaper motto: never let the facts get in the way of a good story.

In a more concrete example, R. Barker Bausell (2007: 109) uses Occam's razor to compare two possible explanations for why patients report reductions in knee pain after receiving acupuncture:

Explanation 1: The reduction in pain following the insertion of tiny needles in the body is due to those needles modulating the flow of a type of energy (qi) through meridians that are specifically designed for this purpose (somewhat similar to the role of arteries in blood flow) thereby reducing the subject's pain.

Explanation 2: It's the placebo effect.

In making our decision, Bausell invites us to adopt Occam's razor and count up the number of unsupported assumptions. For the first explanation we must assume:

(a) the existence of an unmeasured energy form called qi
(b) an as yet undetected system of meridians through which this qi flows

(c) that the acupuncture needles are in fact capable of affecting this flow

(d) that this altered flow is capable of reducing pain

The second explanation requires us to assume:

(a) that a ceremony (of inserting tiny needles into the body accompanied by promises that such practices have reduced pain for thousands of years) can engender psychological explanations of benefit

(b) that these psychological explanations (or suggestions) can influence our perceptions of the pain we experience (or cause us to imagine that we were experiencing less pain than we really were)

Using Occam's razor, then, combined with a large body of evidence for the analgesic placebo effect, we would be guided towards the second explanation.

Applying Occam's Razor to pretentious art descriptions

Illustration 8.2

Tip 57: Beware of 'meaningless' statements

In February 1968, the Beatles went to study transcendental meditation with the Indian guru Maharishi Mahesh in India. A journalist present at the time recounts:

They used to get together in a big hall in the evening and sing songs, and the Maharishi would give them a lecture which would proceed on the following lines: 'When we're delving into the meaning of the Raga you come up with those nether regions which are beyond the stellar spaces, which are so transcendental…' And the more incomprehensible he became the greater was the ecstasy and the rapture on the faces of the audience – including the Beatles.

(*Bombay's Beatle*, BBC Radio 4, 9 August 2009, available at www.bbc.co.uk/programmes/b00hv1dt)

In the 1930s there was a movement in philosophy called 'logical positivism'. Its target was so-called metaphysical statements like those attributed to the Maharishi above. For a statement to be meaningful, the logical positivists argued, it should be possible to show that it's true or false. If we can't, then it should be dismissed as 'meaningless'. Here's an example from the philosopher Alfred Ayer (1936):

- 'To say that "God exists" is to make a metaphysical utterance which cannot be either true or false.'
  - o   it is wrong to say that 'God exists' is true
  - o   wrong to say that it is false
  - o   wrong to say, along with the agnostic, that one does not know if it is true or false
  - o   what one should say is that it is meaningless

This approach to language provides an interesting form of attack on woolly, obscure statements which often feature in the more fringe-like subjects of para-psychology and alternative medicine, as, for example, when someone offers to 'balance', 'cleanse' or 'energise' your chakras.

Tip 58: Watch out for Barnum statements

If you look at the palm of your hand, you'll see a line that begins between your thumb and index finger and curves down towards the centre of your wrist. It's called the 'life line' and, according to chiromancers, it can tell you lots of interesting things about your fate. For example, if you notice a break or a fork in the line this indicates a change in your life – perhaps a career break or some other change in lifestyle. You may also see a few lines that cross your lifeline, which signify obstacles in your path, perhaps an accident or an episode of ill health. Take note of where these forks and crosses occur on the lifeline, because that indicates the time in your life when these significant events will happen.

And when you get to the age of 30 or 40 or 50 – wherever the forks or crosses in the line seem to occur – and you do find yourself changing career, moving house, meeting someone (or meeting someone else), you can gaze back into the palm of your hand and it will say 'I told you so'.

Unless, that is, you are a critically aware sceptic. Then you'll say 'Hold on a minute – don't these things happen to everyone throughout their life? Don't we all change jobs, move houses, have relationship problems, go through periods of poor health during our life?' If you did say this, then you'd recognise these as 'Barnum statements', named after the circus promoter P. T. Barnum, who aimed to provide 'something for everyone'.

Imagine that I've conducted a detailed assessment of your personality, using questionnaires and other assessment techniques, such as handwriting analysis, and having analysed all the data, I can now present you with your own detailed personality profile. Here's *your* profile:

> Some of your aspirations tend to be pretty unrealistic. At times you are extroverted, affable, sociable, while at other times you are introverted, wary and reserved. You have found it unwise to be too frank in revealing yourself to others. You pride yourself on being an independent thinker and do not accept others' opinions without satisfactory proof. You prefer a certain amount of change and variety, and become dissatisfied when hemmed in by restrictions and limitations. At times you have serious doubts as to whether you have made the right decision or done the right thing. Disciplined and controlled on the outside, you tend to be worried and insecure on the inside. While you have some personality weaknesses, you are generally able to compensate for them. You have a great deal of unused capacity which you have not turned to your advantage. You have a tendency to be critical of yourself. You have a strong need for other people to like you and for them to admire you.

What do you think – pretty accurate? Most people think so. And that's the problem. This profile, which consists mainly of statements taken from an astrology book, was given to a class of students who each believed that it had been produced for them individually as a result of completing a personality assessment. When asked how accurate it was on a scale of 0 (poor) to 5 (perfect), it received an average rating of 4.26. Sixteen of the 39 students gave it a perfect rating and only five gave it a rating less than 4 (Forer, 1949). I've tried it myself with students and I'm amazed how effective it is. As the psychologist Gordon Allport puts it:

> When the analyst says, 'You have a need for other people to like and admire you,' the subject is likely to say, 'How true! How accurate you are!'. He should of course say, 'Who hasn't?' Similarly glittering and worthless are such diagnoses as, 'You like change and variety and become dissatisfied when hemmed in by restrictions'; 'Security is one of your major goals in life.' Not only do such statements catch all mortals, they are likely to be interpreted in an individual way by each subject to fit his [sic] unique pattern of life, and he therefore credits the diagnostician with an acumen he does not have. (Allport, 1969: 452)

The banalities of these so-called 'Barnum statements' are present in all disciplines, from politics to psychology, but they're particularly prevalent in the pseudosciences, such as astrology, palmistry and graphology, and among spiritualist mediums, especially when conveying messages from 'the dead' (Greasley, 2000a, 2000b).

Tip 59: Have a look at some websites devoted to critical thinking and sceptical inquiry

There are a number of useful websites devoted to critical thinking and sceptical inquiry. I've listed a selection below:

The James Randi Educational Foundation (www.randi.org)

James Randi is a magician famous for investigating people who claim to have psychic or paranormal abilities, e.g. Uri Geller. The Foundation offers a $1 million prize to anyone who can demonstrate psychic, supernatural or paranormal ability of any kind under mutually agreed upon scientific conditions.

The Skeptics dictionary (www.skepdic.com)

This website has lots of articles covering most supernatural, paranormal and pseudoscientific topics (from acupuncture to zombies).

Science-based Medicine (www.sciencebasedmedicine.org)

Science-based Medicine is run by a group of physicians who subject 'unscientific and pseudoscientific health care' practices to critical examination. This is an excellent resource for those studying health-related topics.

Quackwatch (www.quackwatch.com)

This is another excellent resource for students in the health sciences. It includes articles on health-related frauds, myths, fads, fallacies and misconduct. There's also a link to 'the quackometer' where you can type in the name of someone (e.g. Prince Charles) and it will provide you with a quack rating.

summary

In this chapter we've seen the importance of reaching beyond the lower levels of description that we saw in Bloom's taxonomy towards a more analytical, critical, evaluative perspective, through which an argument is developed and a particular position adopted.

There are some philosophers and psychologists who argue that we are born with a predisposition to believe what we are told, and that we wander around in a kind of hypnotic state with blind belief and uncritical obedience (Schumaker, 1990). As an influential leader once remarked: 'What good fortune for those in power that people do not think' (Adolf Hitler, cited in Macedo, 1994: 36).

One of the primary aims of a university education is to teach students to think critically about what they are told. Perhaps this is what the psychologist B. F. Skinner meant when he said: 'Education is what survives when what has been learned has been forgotten' (Skinner, 1964: 484). So when the 'facts' you learned about your subject at university have been long forgotten, you should hopefully retain the intellectual skills and abilities that encourage you to adopt a critical perspective rather than just accept what you are told. This is important because, as the Princeton philosopher Professor Harry G. Frankfurt (2005: 1 and 63) points out:

> One of the most salient features of our culture is that there is so much bullshit. Everyone knows this. Each of us contributes his share. But we tend to take the situation for granted …

> Bullshit is unavoidable whenever circumstances require someone to talk without knowing what he is talking about. Thus the production of bullshit is stimulated whenever a person's obligations or opportunities to speak about some topic exceed his knowledge of the facts that are relevant to that topic. This discrepancy is common in public life, where people are frequently impelled – whether by their own propensities or by the demands of others – to speak extensively about matters of which they are to some degree ignorant.

9

The greatest source of 'marker distress': language, grammar and expression

> Recent graduates ... seem to have no mastery of the language at all. They cannot construct a simple declarative sentence, either orally or in writing. They cannot spell common, everyday words. Punctuation is apparently no longer taught. Grammar is a complete mystery to almost all recent graduates.
>
> (Complaint about students made in 1961; cited in Pinker, 2014)

In the survey of tutors, problems with language, grammar and expression were listed as the most common source of marker distress. And when the tutors were specifically asked, 'what's the worst thing a student can do in an assignment?', 'poor language, grammar and expression' came a close second after 'failing to answer the question'. Paying a great deal of attention to how you write your assignment is, then, very important. In this chapter we'll be looking at:

- the importance of rewording and editing your text to make it clear and concise
- Grice's 'maxims of conversation' to ensure that what you say clearly expresses what you think (not *always* a good idea ...)
- how to avoid being nominated for the Bad Writing contest
- some common spelling and punctuation mistakes

There's also advice about the use of quotations, acronyms, writing in the impersonal voice, and dangling modifiers.

Tip 60: Good writing is achieved through re-writing

The French philosopher Blaise Pascal (1623–1662), once prefaced a letter with the following apology: 'I didn't have time to write a short letter, so I wrote a long one instead' – the point being that it takes extra effort to produce a document that is concise and to the point. But, as the comments from the survey of tutors emphasise, this is what you need to do in your assignments.

What tutors like

- Concise and articulate writing
- Clarity of writing, making it easy for me to read and follow
- Well written - clear, lucid and meaningful expression. No fluff, just lots of relevant, well-referenced points that connect and form a greater whole

What tutors dislike

- Lack of clarity and obfuscation
- Obfuscation: use of obscure language that fails to communicate in simple terms what the topic is about

Spending time rewriting your work is important, since your first attempt will rarely be the optimum way of communicating ideas. The art of writing is a skill, which is learned with practice, but as with most things, it's probably 5% talent and 95% time and effort: *good writing is achieved through rewriting*. Box 9.1 provides an example of how a rather wordy paragraph might be revised to make it more clear and concise.

box 9.1

How to make a paragraph more concise

In the following example, I've revised the original text to make it more succinct.

Original version

The research project envisages the significant utilisation of both qualitative and quantitative data collection methods, namely

(Continued)

(Continued)

questionnaire surveys, in-depth interviews, and focus groups. In order to collect, measure, and interpret the data, it is necessary to utilise a number of data analysis methods. It is for the achievement of this necessity that the research project plans to use descriptive and inferential statistics as a set of techniques that organise, summarise, and provide a general overview of the data. The research project will execute these methods of data analysis through an important statistical tool, namely SPSS.

Revised version

In this research project I will be using qualitative and quantitative methods, specifically: questionnaires, interviews and focus groups. The data from the questionnaires will be entered into SPSS (Statistical Package for the Social Sciences), and analysed using descriptive and inferential statistics.

Basically, I've edited the original text by removing unnecessary words and phrases (such as 'envisages the significant utilisation' and 'for the achievement of this necessity') and reduced the number of words by over half to provide a much simpler and succinct passage. Notice also that I've provided an explanation for the acronym SPSS (see Tip 68).

Note: If you're one of those students who complain that they're struggling to get anywhere near the word count because you've 'run out of things to say', then you'll be wanting to work the other way round by *adding* unnecessary words and phrases – waffle. Some other strategies you might consider are to use a larger font size than recommended (or a different font which takes up more room), make the margins abnormally wide, and add an extra line space between paragraphs. ☺

Tip 61: Aim for a high signal-to-noise ratio

When I hear students saying 'I need to find another 500 words for my assignment', my heart sinks. It suggests that they've run out of things to say and are simply looking for ways to increase the word count with 'waffle' or 'padding'. A good assignment, which receives a high mark, will not include waffle, padding or unnecessary repetition: it will have a high signal-to-noise ratio.

Tip 62: Follow Grice's maxims

~~In your efforts to achieve clarity and conciseness~~ In order to be clear and concise, it might help to be aware of Grice's (1975) maxims of conversation – a set of rules that we should abide by if we wish to communicate effectively and efficiently. In Table 9.1 I've listed the maxims, accompanied with comments about their relevance to assignments.

Table 9.1 Grice's maxims of conversation

Grice's conversational maxims	Relevance to assignments
Quantity	
• Say no less than is required	Explain/justify
• Say no more than is required	Don't waffle
Quality:	
• Don't say what you believe to be false	Check your facts
• Don't say things for which you lack evidence	Check supporting evidence
Manner:	
• Be clear	Don't be obscure
• Be specific	Don't be ambiguous
• Be brief	Don't waffle
• Be orderly	Pay attention to structure
Relevance:	
• Be relevant	Only include what's relevant to the case you are making

Fortunately, we don't always abide by these maxims in everyday conversation:

Example: Don't say what you believe to be false?

Girlfriend: Does my bum look big in this?

Boyfriend: Massive.

Tip 63: Assume nothing (the curse of knowledge)

The issue of clarity raises the idea of writing for a particular audience: at what level should you be pitching the assignment? Well, my own advice is to assume as little as possible, making sure that you explain any unfamiliar terms.

Some study skills guides suggest that you should address your assignment to an 'expert audience', but this rings alarm bells for me, especially if the assignment requires you to apply the principles of a theory or a model to a context that may be unfamiliar to your tutor. But even when you are discussing subject matter that your tutor knows well, it's still important to provide a clear account to demonstrate your knowledge of the subject. So my advice would be to make your assignment accessible to as wide an audience as possible, otherwise it may come back riddled with question marks and requests for clarification, or be submitted for a prize in a competition (see Box 9.2).

box 9.2

How wonderful to be so profound...

Those who know that they are profound strive for clarity; those who would like to seem profound ... strive for obscurity.

(Friedrich Nietzsche, 1844-1900)

Do you want to impress your tutor with some obscure words in long and complicated sentences demonstrating complex and profound thoughts? Well, don't! Here's an example:

The move from a structuralist account in which capital is understood to structure social relations in relatively homologous ways to a view of hegemony in which power relations are subject to repetition, convergence, and rearticulation brought the question of temporality into the thinking of structure, and marked a shift from a form of Althusserian theory that takes structural totalities as theoretical objects to one in which the insights into the contingent possibility of structure inaugurate a renewed conception of hegemony as bound up with the contingent sites and strategies of the rearticulation of power.

This sentence, from Professor Judith Butler (University of California at Berkeley), won first prize in a competition, the *Bad Writing Contest*, held by the journal *Philosophy and Literature*. It appeared in an article published in the journal *Diacritics* (cited in Lieberman, 2005).

Second prize went to a professor of English at the University of Chicago, Homi Bhabha, for the following sentence (in his *The Location of Culture*, 1994):

If, for a while, the ruse of desire is calculable for the uses of discipline soon the repetition of guilt, justification, pseudo-scientific theories, superstition, spurious authorities, and classifications can be seen as the desperate effort to 'normalize' formally the disturbance of a discourse of splitting that violates the rational, enlightened claims of its enunciatory modality.

Eh?

Why do some people fail to write clearly? Why are most comments on student papers about lack of clarity and the need to explain more? Well, perhaps they are trying to look clever and intellectual like the examples in Box 9.2, or maybe they don't really understand what they're talking about, or maybe they're just not putting enough work into the writing. But another reason is 'the curse of knowledge': our tendency to assume that other people know what we know. For example, if you've ever played charades you'll know how frustrating it is when the audience fails to identify the film you've just been illustrating so clearly and obviously: how could they not see that frantically pointing to your mouth is *Jaws*?

Elizabeth Newton (1990) did an interesting experiment that demonstrates the curse of knowledge. She asked people to tap out the rhythm to popular songs like 'Happy Birthday to You' and see how long it took listeners to identify the song. The 'tappers' believed that the listeners would identify the songs about 50% of the time, but it turned out that they were only correct 1 out of 40 times.

So always try to bear in mind that whoever is reading your assignment will not be as immersed in it as you have been, and explain things clearly.

Tip 64: Check you're spelling, grammar and punctuation

Dr Bernard Lamb, a tutor at Imperial College London and member of the Queen's English Society, collects spelling, grammar and punctuation mistakes made by his students and then publishes them in the newspapers so we can all be outraged at the declining standards in British universities. They include confusing 'compliment' and 'complement', 'holy' and 'holey', 'way' and 'weigh', and 'seamen' and 'semen' (Lamb, 2007):

'the gene products compliment each other'

'holy cheese' [for a cheese with holes]

'have to way up the costs'

'insemination of these cows at the age of 3 with their fathers [*sic*] seamen'

Problems with punctuation included missing apostrophes, for example, 'its' rather than 'it's' (for 'it is') or, as in the above example, 'fathers' rather than 'father's' (each cow presumably only had one biological 'father'). Incidentally, the '[*sic*]' in this quote has been inserted after 'fathers' to indicate that the mistake (the missing apostrophe) was in the original quote – it is not the author's oversight.

Lack of attention to spelling, grammar and punctuation will not only give a poor impression of you as a writer, it may also confuse and frustrate the marker who is trying to read your assignment. As Dr Lamb (1998) points out: 'Spelling is important. Bad spelling gives the impression that the writer is ignorant, careless and unintelligent. It can mislead, confuse and frustrate the reader, and delay or prevent comprehension.' Not a good thing to do to someone who is marking your assignment.

These were some of the most common concerns in the survey of tutors:

What tutors dislike

- Lack of spell-checking and proofreading
- Work not spell-checked (just lazy - it's one click of a button)
- Incorrect use of words, particularly mixing up 'their' and 'there', 'were' and 'where', 'been' and 'being'
- 'It's' when it should be 'its'
- Poor/lack of any proofreading leaving careless mistakes and unreadable sentences - for example, I've encountered discussion about patients who've had cancer of the bowl
- Incorrect use of colons and semicolons

What makes these issues particularly distressing is the fact that many of the errors are easy to address, either by using a spell-checker or proofreading the document prior to submission.

Some common problems

Should it be a colon or a semicolon?

Incorrect use of colons and semicolons is a common problem. My *Concise Oxford Dictionary* defines them as follows:

> Semicolon: a punctuation mark (;) of intermediate value between a comma and a full-stop.

> Colon: a punctuation mark (:) used especially to introduce a quotation or a list of items or to separate clauses when the second expands or illustrates the first.

So, you would use a colon as I have done above (after 'defines them as follows') to introduce a list. Unfortunately, many students use the semicolon instead, which is wrong. You would use a semicolon to link two clauses without connecting words, as in the following example:

> The reader shouldn't turn the page and suddenly be confronted with a figure floating in the air; introduce the figure in the text and then explain it.

Should the full stop go before, or after, the quotes?

Although this cannot be considered one of the most important issues of our age, it is a common problem and, to be honest, something that I was never quite sure about myself. So which is right: (a) or (b)?

a. According to Smith (2015), 'the full-stop should be placed after the quotes'.

b. According to Jones (2015), 'the full-stop should be placed before the quotes.'

The answer depends on which side of 'the pond' you are. It's the Americans who insist on placing the full-stop before the quotes, as in (b), and the reasoning is that it looks nicer tucked away inside the quotes – even if it isn't logical! As Steven Pinker (2014) points out: 'Long ago some American printer decided that the page looks prettier without all the ugly white space above and to the left of a naked period or comma, and we've been living with the consequences ever since.'

Uh oh. But that last sentence has the full-stop before the quotes! Well that's because in this case the full stop is closing the quoted sentence which started with a capital letter. As Lynne Truss (2007: 155) concludes: 'The basic rule is straightforward and logical: when the punctuation relates to the quoted words it goes inside the inverted commas; when it relates to the sentence, it goes outside. Unless, of course, you are in America.'

Is it 'which' or 'that'?

I have just spent a couple of hours comparing a batch of <u>assignments which</u> were awarded a 2:1 with those that were awarded a 1st. What was the difference?

| assignments, which |
| assignments that |
| Ignore |
| Grammar... |

Figure 9.1 Is it 'which' or 'that'?

One of the most common and annoying corrections that my word processor highlights when I'm writing relates to the use of 'which' or 'that' (see, for example, Figure 9.1). This is because 'which' should be used to introduce an optional element to a sentence that may be removed without changing the sense, as in:

Telephone message from garage

Your car, which is an awful colour by the way, has been fixed and is ready for you to collect.

So the reason why my sentence was highlighted is that the element prefaced by 'which' wasn't optional – it was necessary for the sense of the sentence, so it should have been 'that'.

Common comma problems

According to a review by Lunsford and Lunsford (2008), problems with commas account for more than a third of all language errors in student papers, and I suppose we can't discuss them without reference to Lynne Truss's book on punctuation, *Eats, Shoots & Leaves*. The book is prefaced by the following joke:

A panda walks into a café. He orders a sandwich, eats it, then draws a gun and fires two shots in the air.

'Why?' asks the confused waiter, as the panda makes towards the exit. The panda produces a badly punctuated wildlife manual and tosses it over his shoulder.

'I'm a panda,' he says, at the door. 'Look it up.'

The waiter turns to the relevant entry and, sure enough, finds an explanation.

'**Panda**. Large black-and-white bear-like mammal, native to China. Eats, shoots and leaves.' (Truss, 2007)

Before I read this book I actually thought the phrase 'eats, shoots and leaves' was a joke about something else, but I see this makes more sense.

Commas have three main functions:

(a) To separate items in a list

(b) To indicate a non-essential, but interesting, piece of information (bracketing)

(c) To join together two complete sentences

Listing – in place of 'and' or 'or'

Example: There were apples, pears, oranges, and grapes.

Now I expect you're thinking, well, this is obvious; you don't need to bother telling me this. But there is one thing in this sentence that is not obvious – and that's the final comma before the 'and'. It's known as the 'serial comma', and it should be included to avoid potential ambiguity, as in:

Highlights of Peter Ustinov's global tour include encounters with Nelson Mandela, an 800-year-old demigod and a dildo collector.

Bracketing

The comma functions like a bracket to indicate you are providing non-essential information, as in the example cited above: 'Your car, which is an awful colour by the way, has been fixed and is ready for you to collect.'

Joining

A comma can join two complete sentences together and should be followed by 'and', 'or', 'but', 'yet', etc. For example: 'Proofreading your assignment for grammatical errors may be tedious and time-consuming, but it will certainly improve the mark.'

And this brings us on to the most common mistake: using a comma to join two independent clauses that either require a connecting word (conjunction), a semicolon, or may be written as two separate sentences, for example:

People sometimes make the mistake of using a comma at the close of a sentence and then continuing with another sentence that is partly linked, they should really be inserting a semicolon or starting a new sentence.

This is popularly known as the 'comma splice'. For short sentences like the one above the solution is quite simple – start a new sentence or use a semicolon (but longer extracts may need rewriting):

> People sometimes make the mistake of using a comma at the close of a sentence and then continuing with another sentence that is partly linked. They should really be inserting a semicolon or starting a new sentence.

> People sometimes make the mistake of using a comma at the close of a sentence and then continuing with another sentence that is partly linked; they should really be inserting a semicolon or starting a new sentence.

There's a lot more that can be said about the conventions of punctuation, grammar and how to write generally. I've listed a couple of useful websites below:

Learnhigher (Centre for Excellence in Teaching and Learning)

Available at: http://www.learnhigher.ac.uk/writing-for-university/academic-writing/ (accessed April 2015)

University of Toronto Advice on Academic Writing

Available at: http://www.writing.utoronto.ca/advice (accessed April 2015)

Incidentally, when I asked a group of students in the transition from school to university to list features of a poor assignment, the written comments included:

- 'poor spelling and grammer'
- 'poor spelling/grammer/punctuality'

Tip 65: Avoid very long paragraphs (and very short ones)

How to distress tutors

- Paragraphs which are far too short (or too long): for example, paragraphs consisting of one or two sentences or, at the other extreme, the absence of paragraphs

How to impress tutors

- Attention to paragraphing - I loathe whole-page paragraphs!
- When the author understands when to start a new paragraph

A paragraph should contain one idea, a point you are making. Try to keep each paragraph to less than half a page and more than three sentences. A page full of one- or two-sentence paragraphs usually signals a problem in structure.

Table 9.2 Paragraph structure

Typical Structure of a Paragraph
1 The first sentence introduces the subject/topic of the paragraph
2 The following sentences expand/develop the topic
3 The last sentence concludes the paragraph (or perhaps leads into the next paragraph)

Paragraphs can take many different forms, but they are basically structured as outlined in Table 9.2. The paragraph below, in Tip 66, provides a short, but succinct, illustration of this. The first sentence introduces the subject (bullet points), the issue raised about using bullet points is expanded on in the following sentences, and the final sentence concludes with 'So …'.

Tip 66: Don't lapse into listing

Listing bullet points can be a good way to present information clearly, but be careful not to use this as a substitute for discussion in the text. As one tutor in the survey complained: 'Presenting lots of bullet points instead of discussion'. Remember, it's discussion that gets the marks, not bullet points. So, make sure you introduce the list of bullet points in the text and then add some reflective comments directly after the list.

Tip 67: Avoid using too many direct quotes – especially long quotes

How to distress tutors

- Overlong direct quotations
- Filling the assignment with lots of quotes - rather than paraphrasing
- Too many direct quotes when they should be putting things into their own words
- Quotes included but no page numbers given

Quotations should be used in moderation, and only where they are relevant to enhance a point you are making. They shouldn't be used as a substitute for your own interpretation of ideas, especially where the information you are quoting is not saying anything you couldn't have said yourself. If they are used extensively, this can give the impression of laziness – that it has been easier to simply copy the text from somewhere else. So, it's often better to paraphrase the text in your own words and 'originalise' it with your own interpretation and perspective, and reference the source. If you're not sure what 'paraphrasing' is, Box 9.3 provides an illustration.

One of the worst things you can do in an assignment is to copy and paste a few quotations and then just add a few linking sentences as a bridge between them. If quotations are included they should be discussed, analysed and reflected upon.

box 9.3

Paraphrasing: how to do it and how not to do it

When you come across a passage of text that you want to use in your assignment, you can either copy it as a quote or paraphrase it in your own words. If you simply copy the text as a quote, then it needs to be referenced, including the page number from where the quote was taken (see Chapter 10, Box 10.1). But since we know that tutors don't like to see lots of quotes in assignments, it's usually better to paraphrase the text by putting it in your own words – remembering to acknowledge the source, since this shows that you have been reading the relevant literature. In the example below I've paraphrased the main passage in Tip 67.

Original text

Quotations should be used in moderation, and only where they are relevant to enhance a point you are making. They shouldn't be used as a substitute for your own interpretation of ideas, especially where the information you are quoting is not saying anything you couldn't have said yourself. If they are used extensively, this can give the impression of laziness – that it's been easier to simply copy the text from somewhere else. So, it's often better to paraphrase the text in your own words and 'originalise' it with your own interpretation and perspective, and reference the source.

Paraphrase

Quotes can be important in an assignment when they are used to illustrate a point, but some students use them too much when they should be paraphrasing, using their own words. Using too many quotes can give an impression of laziness from the tutor's perspective (Greasley, 2016).

Paraphrasing is about summarising in your own words the essence of what was said. It's *not* about changing a few words here and there, like those highlighted below:

Quotations should be **employed** in moderation, and **just when** they are relevant to **make** a point. They **should not** be used as a substitute for your own interpretation, **particularly** where the information **quoted** is not saying anything you couldn't have said

(Continued)

> *(Continued)*
>
> yourself. If **quotes** are used **a lot** this **gives** the impression of laziness – that it's easier to **just** copy the text from **someone** else. So, it's **usually** better to paraphrase the text in your own words, and reference the source.
>
> I've highlighted the substituted words to give you the tutor's view of this passage when he runs it through the plagiarism software that virtually all universities are using today (see Chapter 11).

Tip 68: Explain all acronyms and TLAs

Tutors were distressed by

- Acronyms used without full explanations being given first
- Not giving a glossary for TLAs

This is a common problem in assignments, partly reflecting an assumption by the student that the tutor who is marking the assignment will be familiar with acronyms and abbreviations. This may or may not be the case, but either way you should always provide an explanation with the *first use* of an acronym or abbreviation (as I added earlier, in Box 9.1, for SPSS). Now obviously there are some acronyms that you might get away with (e.g. BBC, USA, DNA, KFC), but if you think there's a chance that the marker won't know what the acronym stands for, spell it out in the first instance. (See how annoying it is: Three-Letter Abbreviations.)

Tip 69: No person preferred

When writing academic essays and reports you should usually opt for the 'impersonal' voice rather than 'first person' or the rather cumbersome 'third person singular':

- I conducted a literature review ... (first person)
- The author conducted a literature review ... (third person singular)
- A literature review was conducted ... (impersonal)

This may depend on the assignment and the preferences of your tutor, but unless it requires an account from your personal experience, the impersonal voice is usually preferred.

Tip 70: Avoid colloquial language and clichés like the plague

Assignments should be written using a formal style of language rather than the more chatty 'colloquial' language of everyday conversation. Here are two examples which appeared in an assignment (I've highlighted the offending words):

Whether osteopathy can be integrated into the NHS alongside *the likes of* physiotherapy and occupational therapy is debatable ...

It *comes across* that osteopathy was developed with sound medical thought ...

In the first example, 'the likes of' may simply be removed or replaced by 'treatments such as'; in the second example, 'It comes across' might be replaced with 'It would appear'. Warburton (2007) provides a more extreme illustration of colloquial language in the following extract.

Essay question: What were the main causes of the First World War?

At the end of the day, the First World War was the last century's biggest fiasco. A real mudbath, with the generals making a dog's dinner of the tactics and bottling some serious decisions. You may well ask what caused this pig's ear of a war. There were several dodgy things going on at the time ...

Tip 71: Watch out for dangling modifiers

If you have any dangling modifiers they'll need to be rephrased. For example:

Even though he was inebriated, the tutor agreed to see the student.

Who was inebriated – the tutor or the student? The meaning is left 'dangling'.

Tip 72: Read it out loud?

This tip was suggested to me by another tutor, and I initially thought it was a bit naff ('really, like I'm going to read it out loud to myself'), but then I noticed it was recommended by a few famous authors when asked to provide their writing tips in the *Guardian* (20 February 2010). So, if writing well-constructed flowing sentences is not your strong point (perhaps it's been pointed out in feedback on previous assignments?), try reading what you've written out loud to yourself (or to someone else if they'll listen). If nothing else, this will ensure that you're putting some time and effort into checking that your assignment reads well, remembering that this was the *number 1* source of marker distress. The problem is, of course, that most of us don't want to go over what we've written because it probably means more work. It's a bit like examining the ceiling after you've just painted it.

summary

All marking schemes allocate a percentage of the marks to language, grammar and expression. It may only be 10-20% of the overall mark, but this can have a significant impact on the grade: in borderline cases this may be the difference between a fail and a pass, an A and a B. But if an assignment is difficult to understand and follow, this inability to communicate clearly will have a more profound effect on the grade. It may be difficult to gauge the real impact of these factors on the mark, but if they do cause frustration, and certainly if they prevent comprehension, this may be quite substantial.

How you communicate using written language is not just important for university assignments - it's also important in 'real life'. For example, one survey found that 'written communication skills are among the least satisfactory attributes of graduates' (Winch and Wells, 1995: 76). Employers expect high standards of accuracy in written communication, so your employment prospects may depend on your mastery of these skills. A written application form is the first impression a prospective employer has of you. Here's what one employer (Wiens, 2012) wrote about the matter in the *Harvard Business Review*:

> If you think an apostrophe was one of the 12 disciples of Jesus, you will never work for me. ...

> Everyone who applies for a position at either of my companies ... takes a mandatory grammar test. Extenuating circumstances aside (dyslexia, English language learners, etc.), if job hopefuls can't distinguish between 'to' and 'too,' their applications go into the bin. ...

> On the face of it, my zero tolerance approach to grammar errors might seem a little unfair. After all, grammar has nothing to do with job performance, or creativity, or intelligence, right?

> Wrong. If it takes someone more than 20 years to notice how to properly use 'it's,' then that's not a learning curve I'm comfortable with. ...

> Grammar signifies more than just a person's ability to remember high school English. I've found that people who make fewer mistakes on a grammar test also make fewer mistakes when they are doing something completely unrelated to writing - like stocking shelves or labeling parts. ...

> I hire people who care about those details. Applicants who don't think writing is important are likely to think lots of other (important) things also aren't important. And I guarantee that even if other companies aren't issuing grammar tests, they pay attention to sloppy mistakes on résumés. After all, sloppy is as sloppy does.

Incidentally, did you notice the oddly placed commas inside the quotes? American, you see.

10

Referencing - an academic fetish for the anally retentive?

Stealing from one source is plagiarism, but stealing from many sources is research.

(Anon)

These are easy marks to lose or gain.

(Comment from a tutor cited in Greasley and Cassidy, 2010)

Although I'm slightly embarrassed to admit it, I attended a conference on 'referencing in higher education' (held at the University of Bradford in 2009). Thankfully, however, it turned out to be more interesting than it sounds. In one of the sessions, the author Peter Levin suggested that the following definitions (both from the *Concise Oxford Dictionary*) might be of relevance:

Fetish: 1. A thing abnormally stimulating or attracting sexual desire. 2. A thing evoking irrational devotion or respect.

Anally retentive: Excessively orderly and fussy (supposedly owing to aspects of toilet-training in infancy).

Well, these are a fair summary of how some academics look at referencing (though hopefully not the sexual desire).

In this chapter we'll start by looking at the potential impact of poor referencing on your mark, before discussing some of the problems highlighted in the survey of tutors – remember, it was the second most common problem in assignments. Finally, I've included a 'spot the problems' referencing quiz. (Could it get more exciting than this?)

Tip 73: Don't underestimate the impact that referencing can have on your mark

Consider the following scenario. The marker settles down to read your assignment and a few lines into the first page he encounters the first reference in the text. So, he flips to the back of the assignment to locate the reference and finds:

(a) the reference is there, in alphabetical order and fully referenced according to the guidelines provided by the university

(b) the reference is there, in the appropriate place, but it's not complete or it's formatted incorrectly, e.g. missing page numbers for a journal or edited chapter, missing publisher for a book

(c) the reference is not there

As you might imagine: (a) will leave a good impression, (b) will signal potential problems and (c) will set the alarm bells ringing,

While he's there, rummaging around the rear of your assignment, he may take the opportunity to browse through all the references, checking to see that they look OK – that they're formatted according to the guidelines with all the relevant information. If this is the case, then things are looking good and he may not pay too much attention to the references here on in. However, if (b) or (c) is the case, he will reach for the red pen. Having located a problem with the first reference, he will then go through the references with a fine-toothed comb checking for similar problems with other references.

Problems with referencing can affect the marks in two ways:

1. Directly - marks are simply deducted for referencing on the relevant part of the mark sheet. This may constitute around 10% of the marks.

2. Indirectly (and more 'globally') due to a *poor initial impression* - if this student can't even be bothered to follow guidelines for referencing (as one tutor noted in the survey), then what else couldn't they be bothered to do?

So if you are unable to master the detailed pedantic intricacies of referencing (or simply can't be bothered), you might do well to remember that this oversight may have a more *global* impact on how your assignment is perceived.

Tip 74: Check for missing references

One of the main problems identified in the survey was missing references. There's nothing more frustrating than turning to the back of the essay only to find that the reference is missing (particularly the first reference), as the following comments from the tutors' survey highlight:

How to distress tutors

- References that don't appear in reference list [and references appearing in the list but not cited]

- Careless referencing, e.g. where not proofread to make sure all authors cited are on reference list

- Lack of attention to referencing - particularly when the first reference is missing or incomplete - a very bad sign!

So whatever you do, make sure all the references you've cited in the text are present.

My own strategy when I've finished writing something is to tick each reference in the text when I've checked that it is also in the references section (some tutors actually do this when marking assignments). It's a tedious task, for sure, but if you want a high mark, getting the referencing right is not something tutors are impressed by – it's what they expect.

Tip 75: Check for incomplete references

Once you have checked that all the references cited in the assignment are present, the next task is to ensure that they have all the necessary information – since *incomplete references* were another bane in markers' lives:

How to distress tutors

- Author cited and no date

- Bad referencing - anything from missing page numbers, misspelled author names, etc. ...

Common problems include: absence of the publisher and place of publication for books; missing page numbers for chapters in edited books; omitting volume number and page numbers for journal articles.

Tip 76: Use references within the text to support your statements

When it comes to referencing within the text (rather than the list of references at the end of an assignment), a common problem highlighted in the survey of tutors was failing to reference sources of information.

What tutors dislike

- Arguments not referenced properly (e.g. no references)
- Statements, evidence, etc. without any references

There are some students who tend to 'under-reference' in their assignments – forgetting to cite relevant sources that they have consulted. But it's important to remember that evidence of reading and investigation is a crucial element for assignments and will be a significant factor in the marking criteria. So when you look through the first draft of your assignment, check to make sure that you have included references to the literature you have been reading.

Referencing is particularly important when you are discussing specific claims based on evidence from research studies. For example, the following passage makes several claims about the effectiveness of homeopathic treatments but manages to conceal the sources of these claims excellently:

> Homeopathic treatment has been proven effective in treating several conditions, whether acute or chronic illnesses. Aconite and Bryonia are used to effectively treat colds and influenza. Influenza sufferers were shown to recover twice as quickly when taking homeopathic remedies in a double-blind study. Numerous studies published in the *BMJ* confirm the effectiveness of homeopathic remedies for rheumatoid arthritis, diabetes, infections, circulatory problems, depression, respiratory problems, heart disease, nervous disorders, headaches, and allergies. Homeopathy has also been used to help the healing process after surgery or chemotherapy.

Exercise: Inserting reference

There are a number of places where references should be inserted in the above passage. Make a note yourself before turning to the end of this chapter to see where they should be.

Tip 77: Use 23 references for every 2,000 words

It's not uncommon for students to ask 'how many references should I be citing in my assignment?', to which I usually respond '23'. This is a joke of course (though it's surprising how many students write it down). There should be as many references as are required for your particular assignment, bearing in mind that the number of references you do cite will reflect the breadth of your reading. However, remember that tutors value argument over coverage – depth rather than breadth (write a lot about a little, rather than a little about a lot).

Tip 78: Don't spoil the ship for a ha'p'orth of tar

A study by Neville (2009b) suggests that one of the reasons why students fail to reference properly is time-management issues. Here are a few complaints from the students – along with my own thoughts (in italics):

It's hugely time-consuming and a real pain. (Undergraduate: English Literature)

Yes it is. I totally agree.

More time ends up being spent on checking the references than the work itself – which is ridiculous! (Foundation Studies student)

Perhaps this says more about the amount of time this student has spent on their assignment.

It can take a good portion of the day to perfect it ... therefore one disadvantage is that it can be time-consuming and may put people off. (Undergraduate: Law and Politics)

Yes, it can take a good portion of the day to check the references: students who receive high marks accept this. Students who put the time and effort into their assignments to get a high mark usually put the time into referencing properly (as the saying goes, you don't want to spoil the ship for a ha'p'orth of tar).

Tip 79: **There will be guidelines on how to reference - consult them**

The study by Neville (2009b) also included the following complaints:

It's taught very quickly and glossed over by academics who have done it for so many years, leaving students clueless and inevitably getting it wrong.'

'Even though I'm in my third and final year, I still don't understand how to reference properly.' (Undergraduate: Law)

Well, here's an idea, you could use your initiative and find out for yourself. Problems with referencing are particularly annoying since there are so many guidelines available to students.

How to distress tutors

- Lack of ability to reference (in spite of the handout)
- Inaccurate referencing, despite all the guidance available
- Failing to reference or failing to reference/cite correctly despite being given an assignment guide which details how to reference and cite every possible type of source

Guidelines on how to reference in the appropriate format should be available from your tutor and the library. Get a copy, the sooner the better.

Tip 80: **One list to rule them all**

Sometimes a student will decide to present different types of reference in separate lists at the end of the assignment: one list for books, another for journal articles, and another for internet sources. This might seem like a good idea, but there are two problems. First, it's difficult to tell from the reference in the text which list the marker should be looking at to locate the reference. Second, it's not following guidelines: all the references should be in one list ordered alphabetically.

Tip 81: References are not the same as a bibliography

Did you know that there's a difference between a references section and a bibliography? (Do you care?) A bibliography is all the references you have consulted when researching your assignment – whether or not they have been referred to in the text of your assignment. A references section should only contain those references actually cited in the text. Most assignments will require you to just list the references you have cited in the text.

Tip 82: Referencing: these are easy marks to lose or gain

It's relatively easy for tutors to glance through the references section and spot errors (like shooting fish in a barrel). If they do this early on, and the first reference is wrong or missing, it will not leave a good first impression. If they spot errors at the end, it will leave a poor last impression. So, time spent checking that your references are (a) all present, (b) contain all the necessary details, and (c) are presented in the correct format stipulated in the guidelines is important. The 5% you lose on the mark sheet due to poor referencing could make the difference between a pass and a fail or an A and a B. These are easy marks to lose or gain.

Tip 83: You could 'cite as you write' using bibliographic software

You may wish to use bibliographic software to manage your references. For example, there's a facility in Microsoft Word which enables you to 'cite as you write'. You start by putting the cursor where you want the reference to be inserted in the text, then click on the *References* tab and *Insert Citation/Add New Source* where you select the type of reference it is (book, journal, etc.) and complete the details (author, title, etc.). This creates a database of references which can then be inserted at the end of your assignment. But ensure they are in the format specified by your tutor.

Tip 84: Check for inconsistencies between references cited in the text and those in the reference list ('do as I say, not as I do')

This tip was suggested by the professional copyeditor from SAGE who had the unfortunate task of copyediting this book prior to publication. Admittedly, there were a few minor 'oversights', including some missing references, quotes without page numbers, inconsistent dates and author spellings, incomplete details, and a handful of surplus references that were not actually cited in the text (which all goes to show the importance of conducting a thorough check!).

A really quick guide to referencing

It is beyond the scope of this book to provide a comprehensive guide to referencing (which is a shame, because I would have so loved to detail the intricate minutiae of referencing styles), and in any case, you should obtain a copy of the referencing guidelines provided by your own university. However, since the 'author–date' method of referencing is the favoured approach in the social sciences, Box 10.1 provides a really quick guide using the main types of reference:

- Journal article
- Book
- Book chapter (also an example of what to do with multiple (three or more) authors)
- Website
- Government report

box   10.1

An example of how to reference using the author-date method

Main text

Research has shown that one of the most common problems in student assignments is the quality of referencing (Greasley and Cassidy, 2010; Centre for Referencing Standards, 2009). According to Greasley and Cassidy (2010), the main problems are:

> not following guidelines about correct formatting ('despite all the guidance available') and incomplete or missing references. More fundamental problems were also raised in terms of failing to reference within the text (which could lead to plagiarism) and the quality of references, e.g. over-reliance on web/internet sources rather than more reliable sources such as books or journals. (p. 7)

Fortunately, there are now a number of guides and resources to ensure that problems with references will become a thing of the past, with no student failing to reference properly in the future. ☺ These include

(Continued)

(Continued)

books (e.g. Neville, 2007) and a range of online resources, such as those provided by the Centre for Excellence in Teaching and Learning (2009). Your university will also have its own referencing guide that you should consult.

Interestingly, a survey by Norton et al. (1996) found that many students have included a false bibliography (listing sources that were not actually consulted!), to give the impression that they've read more than they actually have, and they have even changed the dates of old research to make it look like up-to-date research. This is, of course, not recommended.

References

Centre for Excellence in Teaching and Learning (2009) *Referencing*. Available at: www. learnhigher.ac.uk (accessed 25 January 2016)

Centre for Referencing Standards (2009) *Academic Pedantry and Tedium in Higher Education*. London: Higher Education Authority.

Greasley, P. and Cassidy, A. (2010) When it comes round to marking assignments: how to impress and how to distress lecturers.... *Assessment & Evaluation in Higher Education*, 35(2): 173-189.

Neville, C. (2007) *The Complete Guide to Referencing and Avoiding Plagiarism*. Maidenhead: Open University Press.

Norton, L.S., Dickins, T.E. and McLaughlin Cook, N. (1996) Coursework assessment: what are tutors really looking for? In G. Gibbs (ed.), *Improving Student Learning: Using Research to Improve Student Learning*. Oxford: Oxford Centre for Staff Development, Oxford Brookes University (pp.155-166).

There are just a few points to notice about the referencing in Box 10.1.

Page numbers for quotes

First, if you do insert a quote, it must have page numbers (assuming it's from a book or a journal, rather than a source such as the internet). I have provided the page numbers for the quote *after* the quote. Sometimes guidelines may suggest inserting page numbers within the reference. For example: 'According to Greasley and Cassidy (2010, p. 7), the main problems...'. Either way, the crucial point is to include the page numbers so that the quote can be located by the reader.

The quote included in the box is indented

Since this is quite a long quote, I have chosen to present it as an indented passage of text. This is recommended if the quote is substantial (e.g. three or more sentences, or sometimes a specific word limit may be recommended).

Citing internet sources

Notice that I have used the title of the organisation for the internet reference: Centre for Excellence in Teaching and Learning. This is because there is no personal author; had there been an author, I would have referenced the source under their name, for example:

Smith, J. (2009) *Referencing*. Centre for Excellence in Teaching and Learning. Available at: www.learnhigher.ac.uk/ (accessed 12 January 2016)

The absence of an 'author' (person or organisation) is a common problem when referencing website sources in assignments. So, as the above example illustrates, the important thing is to include an author if the website has one, or if not, use the name of the organisation.

Another fairly common problem is a list of unidentified nameless websites all starting with 'www.'. As noted above, you should always provide an author or organisation to identify a website.

You should also provide the date when you accessed the internet reference (as the above example illustrates), since websites are often updated.

Spot the error: some common referencing problems

In Box 10.2 I've provided a list of references which include some common problems. Can you spot them? Incidentally, they are all genuine articles. In fact, most of them are award winners: The Ig Nobel Prize – organised by the magazine *Annals of Improbable Research* (www.improbable.com/ig/winners).

box   10.2

Referencing – spot the problems

The following references contain a number of deliberate errors. Can you spot them?

1 Glenda Browne (2001) The definite article: acknowledging 'The' in index entries. The Indexer.
2 Cadiergues, M.C., Joubert, C. and Franc, M. (2000) A comparison of jump performances of the dog flea and the cat flea. *Veterinary Parasitology*, volume 92, number (3), October 2000, 239-41.
3 Centre for Excellence in Teaching & Learning (2009) *Referencing*. Available at: www.learnhigher.ac.uk

(Continued)

(Continued)

4 FESMIRE, F. M. (1988) Termination of intractable hiccups with digital rectal massage, <u>Annals of Emergency Medicine</u>, 17(8), 872.

5 Harvey, J. et al. (2002) An analysis of the forces required to drag sheep over various surfaces. *Applied Ergonomics*, 33(6), 523–31.

6 May, P. R. A., Fuster, J. M., Newman, P. and Hirschman, A. (1976) Woodpeckers and head injury, *Lancet*, 307(7957), 454–5.

7 Hong, C.Y., Shieh, C. C., Wu, P. and Chiang, B.N. 1987. *The spermicidal potency of Coca-Cola and Pepsi-Cola.* Human Toxicology, 6(5), 395–6.

8 Norton, L.S., Dickins, T.E and N. McLaughlin Cook (1996) *Coursework assessment: what are tutors really looking for?* In Gibbs, G. (ed) Improving student learning: Using research to improve student learning. Oxford: Oxford Centre for Staff Development, Oxford Brookes University.

9 Sims, D. (2005) "You Bastard: A Narrative Exploration of the Experience of Indignation within Organizations", *Organization Studies*, 26(11): pp.1625–40.

10 Witcombe, Brian and Meyer, Dan (2006) Sword swallowing and its side effects, *BMJ*, 1285–7.

The answers are provided at the end of this chapter.

Note: I have numbered these references for ease of identification; they should not normally be numbered if you are using the author-date style for referencing.

summary

Believe it or not, academics have conducted research to examine the accuracy of references in academic journals. Here are the results from just two of the many studies:

- Faunce and Job (2001) examined 355 references from five experimental psychology journals published by the American Psychological Association: 30% contained errors.

- Foreman and Kirchhoff (1987) examined 17 nursing journals and found an overall error rate of 31%.

The errors were mainly related to author names, article titles, journal volume, page numbers and year of publication.

Now you might be wondering what would possess someone to devote a significant proportion of their precious little time on Earth to research the accuracy of referencing in journals, but this does highlight two important points:

- The importance accorded by academics to accurate referencing
- Getting the references right is not just a problem for students

But if you've ever spent a significant amount of time trying to locate a reference and failed, only to find that you were looking for the wrong author or the wrong volume number, then you will appreciate the importance of accurate references. As Spivey and Wilkes (2004: 281) point out:

> Given the functions references serve, the implications of citation errors are serious. Errors may impede retrieval of background information, call into question the attention given to the construction of the article, and compromise the author's credibility as a researcher.

For the word 'article' in the above quote, substitute 'assignment'.

When it comes to referencing, the main things to keep in mind are the following:

1   Acknowledge your sources in a transparent and consistent manner, providing all the information you would need to locate the reference.
2   Consult and follow the referencing guidelines that are available from your university – to show that you've made the effort. Failure to do this gives the impression that you can't be bothered, and that's why it was listed as the second most annoying problem in the survey of tutors. And who knows the extent to which that impression will influence the marker's perception of you, and your assignment.
3   Keep a record of all your sources used. As one librarian pointed out to a student: 'In a library of over 2 million items it's not always easy to identify "the book with the red cover I borrowed about a month ago".'
4   Compile your reference list as you go. Don't leave it until the end, and then it's not such a tedious task.

Answers to referencing exercises

Exercise: inserting references (see p. 120)

There are five places where references should have been inserted, which I've indicated below:

Homeopathic treatment has been proven effective in treating several conditions, whether acute or chronic illnesses (REF1). Aconite and Bryonia are used to effectively treat colds and influenza (REF2). Influenza sufferers were shown to recover twice as quickly when taking homeopathic remedies in a double-blind study (REF3). Numerous studies published in the *BMJ* confirm the effectiveness of homeopathic remedies for rheumatoid arthritis, diabetes, infections, circulatory problems, depression, respiratory problems, heart disease, nervous disorders, headaches, and allergies (REF4). Homeopathy has also been used to help the healing process after surgery or chemotherapy (REF5).

In each case the reference is required as evidence for the claims that are being made, that is, the reference to the research studies upon which each of these claims is founded.

It's also worth noting here that references should be inserted directly after each statement in order to identify the source of that particular assertion. Sometimes students will simply insert a list of references at the end of the paragraph (so in the above example all five would be listed at the end). The problem is that the reader is not then able to identify which reference relates to which statement.

It may be that a secondary source is being used, that is, an article or book which recounts these claims. If this is the case, the original research study should be presented as 'cited in' the secondary source you are using, for example:

> Homeopathic treatment has been proven effective in treating several conditions, whether acute or chronic illnesses (Smith, 2000, cited in Jones, 2004). Aconite and…

Answers to Box 10.2: referencing – spot the problems

Note: There are many subtle variations in referencing styles (e.g. underlining rather than italicising the journal name), so it's important to consult your own university guidelines. For these references I have been using a system based on the American Psychological Association author–date method, which is one of the most common referencing styles in the social sciences.

1. Glenda Browne (2001) The definite article: acknowledging 'The' in index entries. The Indexer.

   Author surname should be first, and just initial for first name; journal should be italicised; volume number, issue number and page numbers are missing. This is how it should read:

   Browne, G. (2001) The definite article: acknowledging 'The' in index entries. *The Indexer*, 22(3), 119-22.

2. Cadiergues, M.C., Joubert, C. and Franc, M. (2000) A comparison of jump performances of the dog flea and the cat flea. *Veterinary Parasitology*, volume 92, number (3), October 2000, 239-41.

   Remove 'volume', 'number', 'October', and repetition of year of publication '2000'. This is how it should read:

Cadiergues, M.C., Joubert, C. and Franc, M. (2000) A comparison of jump performances of the dog flea and the cat flea. *Veterinary Parasitology*, 92(3), 239-41.

3. Centre for Excellence in Teaching and Learning (2009) *Referencing*. Available at: www.learnhigher.ac.uk

   This just needs the date accessed after the web address: (accessed 12 January 2016).

4. FESMIRE, F.M. (1988) Termination of intractable hiccups with digital rectal massage. Annals of Emergency Medicine, 17(8), 872.

   Inconsistent formatting: author name in capitals and journal underlined rather than italicised like the rest. This style may be recommended in some guidelines but in this case it's not consistent with the style used for the other references.

5. Harvey, J. et al. (2002) An analysis of the forces required to drag sheep over various surfaces. *Applied Ergonomics*, 33(6), 523-31.

   You shouldn't use 'et al.' in the reference list – all authors should be listed (there were six altogether: Harvey, J., Culvenor, J., Payne, W., Cowley, S., Lawrance, M., Stuart, D. and Williams, R.).

   Some guidelines will put a limit on the number of authors you should cite in the reference list, e.g. only list the first three authors, then put 'et al.'. This would be necessary if you were citing an article called 'The Sloan Digital Sky Survey: Technical summary' which appeared in the *Astronomical Journal* (2000) and listed 144 authors!

6. May, P.R.A., Fuster, J.M., Newman, P. and Hirschman, A. (1976) Woodpeckers and head injury. *Lancet*, 307(7957), 454-5.

   The reference is fine – but it's not in alphabetical order.

7. Hong, C.Y., Shieh, C.C., Wu, P. and Chiang, B.N. 1987. *The spermicidal potency of Coca-Cola and Pepsi-Cola*. Human Toxicology, 6(9), 395-6.

   Brackets around the date are missing; the article title rather than the journal is italicised. (This style may be recommended in some guidelines but not the APA that we're following.)

8. Norton, L.S., Dickins, T.E. and N. McLaughlin Cook (1996) *Coursework assessment: what are tutors really looking for?* in Gibbs G. (ed.) Improving student learning: Using research to improve student learning. Oxford: Oxford Centre for Staff Development, Oxford Brookes University.

   The third author's initial should be after their last name; the book title rather than the chapter should be italicised; editor's initial should appear before surname; no page numbers for the chapter are given. This is how it should be:

   Norton, L.S., Dickens, T.E. and McLaughlin Cook, N. (1996) Coursework assessment: what are tutors really looking for? In G. Gibbs (ed.) *Improving student learning: Using research to improve student learning* (pp. 155-166). Oxford: Oxford Centre for Staff Development, Oxford Brookes University.

9. Sims, D. (2005) "You Bastard: A Narrative Exploration of the Experience of Indignation within Organizations", *Organization Studies*, 26(11): pp.1625-40.

Inconsistent formatting: quotation marks and using capitals in the title of the article; a colon rather than a comma has been used after the volume/issue number; and pp. has been used to indicate pages. Your university referencing guide may recommend this formatting, but in this case it's not consistent with the other references.

10. Witcombe, Brian and Meyer, Dan (2006) Sword swallowing and its side effects. *BMJ*, 1285-7.

First names have been included (it should just be initials); journal title has been abbreviated – should be *British Medical Journal*; and volume/issue number is also missing: 333(7582).

11

Plagiarism

This chapter is for students who have a 'poorly developed authorial identity', for example, copying and pasting large chunks of text that someone else has written and pretending you've written it yourself. It's usually referred to as 'plagiarism'. In this chapter we'll look at different ways to commit plagiarism (including plagiarising yourself), the means by which tutors are able to detect it (e.g. using plagiarism detection software), and how to get the cheapest deal if you're paying an essay writing company to write your assignment. And we'll look at the consequences if you're caught.

Cambridge University: a hotbed of plagiarism?

Almost half of students admitted to plagiarism in a poll carried out by a students' newspaper at the University of Cambridge. (*BBC News*, 2008)

This was the opening sentence from a BBC news report in 2008. The figures are based on a survey conducted by the *Varsity* student newspaper at Cambridge University (Stothard, 2008). According to the survey 49% of students had: handed in someone else's essay; copied and pasted from the internet; copied statistics or fieldwork; made up statistics or fieldwork; handed in previously submitted work; used someone else's ideas without acknowledgement; bought an essay, or had an essay edited by Oxbridge Essays (a company offering essays for sale – more on this later).

Tip 85: Know what counts as plagiarism

Plagiarism, in the context of academic writing, is the attempt to pass somebody else's work, ideas or writing as your own. The Cambridge University survey gives some clear examples:

- using someone else's ideas without acknowledgement
- copying sections of text without acknowledging the source

- handing in someone else's essay or work written by someone else

- handing in previously submitted work (plagiarising yourself!)

Students tend to plagiarise in four main ways (Park, 2003: 475):

1. Stealing material from another source and passing it off as their own. For example:

    i. Buying a paper from an essay writing company (pre-written or specially written)

    ii. Copying a whole paper from another source text without proper acknowledgement

    iii. Submitting another student's work, with or without that student's knowledge.[1]

2. Submitting a paper written by someone else (e.g. a peer or relative) and passing it off as their own.

3. Copying sections of material from other sources, including the full reference, but leaving out quotation marks, giving the impression that the material has been paraphrased rather than directly quoted.

4. Paraphrasing material from one or more source texts without supplying appropriate referencing.

In the Cambridge survey it was noted that only 5% of students had actually been caught plagiarising, but it's worth noting that, since plagiarism is such a serious accusation, suspicions may be held about a piece of work without the issue being raised with the student; and if you're under suspicion, that's not a good place to be. It's also interesting to note that 81% of students 'felt the university was proactive enough about defining and punishing plagiarism'. Well, given that only 5% appear to have been caught, they would, wouldn't they?

Tip 86: Plagiarism is 'the most serious act of deception anyone in academic life can be accused of'

Plagiarism has become a serious problem in recent years, with the ability to copy and paste information from the internet and electronic sources. The survey from Cambridge University gives an indication of the scale of the problem, but other sources suggest that plagiarism is widespread, with thousands of students being found guilty each year. For example, using a Freedom of

---

[1]Researchers at the University of Central England discovered an interesting example of this when they found that students were putting their coursework assignments out to tender online, with suppliers bidding to undertake the work! (Baty, 2006; also cited in Naylor, 2007.)

Information request, it was revealed that among just half of British universities there were 6,672 incidents of plagiarism and collusion reported during 2003–2004. At Westminster University 707 students were found to have copied work without declaring it, which was the highest incidence in the survey of 64 higher education institutions (Blair, 2005). As Sally Feldman (2009) pointed out in *Times Higher Education*: 'There's a new bloodsport on Britain's campuses. It's got everything: the thrill of the chase, the lust for blood and the satisfaction of the kill ... its name is plagiarism.'

The penalties can be severe, as the following extract from 'Bradford University guidelines on plagiarism: statement of academic integrity' illustrates:

> Copying assessments breaches academic integrity in a fundamental way and constitutes a grave breach of regulations and as such the University would take necessary disciplinary action. Copying is simply a form of cheating – pretending something is yours when it is not. At its most blatant, it is generally known as plagiarism, the most serious act of deception anyone in academic life can be accused of. But even if there is no deliberate intention to deceive, copying is unacceptable academic practice. For this reason, if you are found to have copied from others in your assessments, you can expect heavy penalties to be imposed upon you. At best you're likely to receive no marks for the piece of work, be asked to complete it again properly and find that you have adversely affected the class of degree you will be awarded. At worst, the penalty may be permanent exclusion from the University.

> Should an investigating committee find you guilty of cheating/copying this will be recorded on your student file. This may have an impact on the future provision of academic references requested by you in the support of continued study or employment and put at risk your career prospects. ...

> The University is committed to ensuring that its academic integrity and standards of academic awards are secure and encourages appropriate use of electronic detection software packages by academic staff and students to combat plagiarism and copying.

These guidelines point out that the university is encouraging the use of electronic detection software packages, such as Turnitin, to combat plagiarism. This software is now well established at most universities and, from my own experience of using it to check student submissions, it is extremely effective in identifying text taken from other sources (e.g. web pages, journals, student papers).

Tip 87: If you pay for someone else to write your assignment, remember, the clues are there

There are quite a few companies providing essays for sale on the internet. A House of Commons report (Innovation, Universities, Science and Skills

Committee, 2009: 122) estimated that 'bespoke writing "services" … are available via more than 250 sites in the UK alone' and that these services are attracting 'spending of more than 200 million pounds per year'. Here's a typical example of how they advertise:

Unbelievable Essays! - helping you get a better degree!

The World's 'original' provider of bespoke essays, dissertations and coursework...

Welcome to **Unbelievable Essays**! We are a company that can provide you with an 'original' answer to your essay (assignment, report, dissertation etc.). Your assignment will be written to a **guaranteed standard** by one of our expert writers. Simply state the grade you would like (ranging from a premium first to a bargain bucket third), and let us do the work. We guarantee the standard requested - or your money back! We even include a **£5,000 no-plagiarism guarantee!**

So make that long list of acerbic comments on your feedback sheet a thing of the past: 'I can't believe it's your essay!' - is what your tutor will say when he calls you in for a chat.

There are lots of companies that will offer to write you a 'custom essay' – for a price. How much? Well it depends on four things:

- How fast do you want it? The standard turnaround time is around 3-4 weeks, but the price increases if you need it more urgently: the quickest delivery I saw was within 3 hours

- The level/type of assignment: school essays are cheaper than undergraduate essays, which are cheaper than master's dissertations, and then there's PhDs

- How many words? 1,000 to 50,000

- What grade you would like? First class, 2:1 or a budget 2:2

When I requested a price for a 2,000-word assignment to be completed within a month, the quotes fell within the range £280–480 (first), £190–365 (2:1) and £140–180 (2:2). It was £3,200 for a 10,000-word postgraduate dissertation.

According to one essay-writing company, overseas students represent almost half their customers – with a rise in demand fuelled by the recruitment of students whose English language skills are poor (Coughlan, 2008). Suspicions are raised, however, when a student who can barely speak English (not necessarily foreign) goes on to submit an assignment which reads like it was written by a Cambridge don – sophisticated language, wide vocabulary and colloquial phrasing. There's also very often a feeling of 'remoteness' from the actual assignment guidelines – which is what you might expect if it's written by somebody who's not attended the course. You can adapt it of course, but then you run into the problems of changes in style – which just adds to the suspicions.

Tip 88: Busy social life? Find reading and writing tedious? Why not pay someone to write your assignment?

Here are a few emails from customers (supposedly) on the website for Custom Research Papers (an essay-writing service: www.customresearchpapers.us/, accessed July 2009):

> I am a part-time student currently pursuing a degree course and working full-time. Hence, it leaves me with little time to research on and to do a well-written essay assignment.

> I'm on a deadline with about four or five papers due. They aren't that tough to do, but I've recently been put on 10 hours a day, seven days a week at work and I'm too exhausted to keep up anymore. Can you help????

> Thank you so much for your EXCELLENT CUSTOMER SERVICE in this matter. … You guys seem to be the real thing to hard working single parent students that need the extra help. Thank you for being there!!!!

So if you're just too busy – and particularly if you're a single parent – the message is that you should feel no guilt about paying for someone else to do your assignment. Here's some more encouragement from the website:

> Would it make a difference in <u>YOUR</u> life, if you could …

- Have more time to handle your overloaded schedule?
- Skip hours of boring and time-consuming writing?
- Waste no more time at libraries searching through piles of books and articles?
- Spend time with your family and see your friends more often?
- Avoid the risk of being spotted in plagiarism?
- Get a good grade for your paper and relax about finishing the course?
- Put the burden of writing frequent research paper assignments on someone else's shoulders?

Alternatively, if you do want to spend more time with your family, 'skip hours of boring and time-consuming writing' and wasting time at libraries and reading books – don't enrol on an academic course.

They even provide a profile of the writers who are 'ready to help you':

Patience Houghly

Patience is a freelance academic writer with 10 years experience. She has written over 200 journal articles on a variety of topics, including Sociology, English Literature, Art, Philosophy and Psychology.

Helena Gipoutchy

Helena has worked for many years as a researcher and lecturer. She gained a first class degree in Psychology before completing a PhD in Education. She has published widely in the fields of psychology, social studies and education.

Pete Greasley

Pete has had a long and undistinguished career in academia. He recently joined our team after coming across the website while researching a book on writing assignments. It's part of his retirement plan.

(Note: I have made up the first two profiles, but names and profiles are provided on some websites.)

Tip 89: Don't be beguiled

It might be argued that demonising these essay-writing services is unfair since they are actually providing additional support and guidance for students that may be lacking from their university (Naylor, 2007). For example, the Oxbridge Essays website (www.oxbridgeessays.com/, accessed January 2010) included a section titled 'Having doubts/Is it cheating?' where the deficiencies of the 'modern British university education' are highlighted: large class sizes, inadequate support/time/attention for students. As such, the service is positioned as a source of support – a form of 'online tutoring':

> Students who ... use our service should feel no guilt whatsoever. What we provide is a form of online tutoring. Very few people object to the idea of private tutoring, and students who arrange such tutoring online are doing essentially the same thing – only through the medium of the internet rather than a face-to-face meeting. Indeed, whilst internet tuition lacks the personal element of a face-to-face tutorial, it is much more economical than expensive private tuition, which makes it available to a far wider spectrum of students.

> We believe that there is a real bravery about those students who refuse to be hampered by the failings of their university and instead take it upon themselves to arrange the professional academic aid that will help them get the degree results and therefore the career opportunities they deserve.

But 'support' is one thing and offering to provide a tailor-made essay to a specific brief is another:

> Our specialised custom essay writing service provides a range of options to meet your academic needs; we can provide you with a tailor-made essay, coursework or college assignments...

Our writing team can work to a specific title or, if you would prefer, they are happy to suggest a title to you after a discussion of your needs…

… your essay will be sourced using the highest quality material; of course, if you wish to have specific sources or material included just let us know and our writers can easily accommodate this…

Just to make things clear: if you provide the company with the specific essay title and brief, and submit the finished article or parts of it as your own work, then this is plagiarism. If you get caught, the penalties may be devastating. I was involved in one incident where the outcome was exclusion from the course.

Tip 90: 'Essay banks' are a cheaper option

'Essay banks', such as Studymode.com (formerly known as Cheathouse) and EssayBank.com, provide thousands of 'sample essays' covering a range of subject areas (e.g. arts, business, history, social sciences). According to EssayBank. com, the essays have been written by 'University teachers, students, and academic experts who have submitted their works to us in exchange for access to our comprehensive database'. Otherwise, you have to pay: £4.99 for a month or £34.99 for a year. At Studymode.com it's a bit more expensive: $9.90 for three days access and $69.90 for six months access (April 2010 prices).

When I searched for an assignment about 'plagiarism' on Cheathouse.com, it retrieved nearly 200 entries. A brief extract of each essay is provided for free, for example:

What is Plagiarism? Plagiarism is a grave concern when discussing ethics in an academic environment. With the introduction of the internet and the World Wide Web many publications are available online and some students use these papers for academic assignments instead of doing research and creating an original essay…

Guidance is provided about the use of these 'sample essays'. For example, Cheathouse.com points out that 'generally, there are no problems using essays, as long as you acknowledge the sources! This is absolutely essential. This means that if you use an idea or if you make a direct quote or you paraphrase from another essay, you must include the essay in your bibliography.' Personally though, I'd think twice about citing www.cheathouse.com in my assignment.

Tip 91: How to avoid plagiarism: acknowledge and/or rephrase

Copying and pasting is the 'zeitgeist of the times', the spirit of the age we live in: if you come across some useful information online, you can simply copy and paste it into your file. However, the important issue, in terms of avoiding plagiarism, is what you do with this information once you've got it. There are basically two options:

1. Rephrase the information in your own words and acknowledge the source even if it's not a direct quote – this shows that you've been reading the literature, which is a significant part of the marking criteria for assignments. Putting things in your own words also forces you to think more about what you're writing and its relevance to your assignment. (See also Box 9.3 which provides an example of how to paraphrase – and how *not* to.)

2. Put quotations around the text and cite the source.

Generally speaking, it's as simple as that, and there's no danger of being charged with plagiarism.

What happens if you're charged with plagiarism?

The procedures for dealing with plagiarism will vary across different universities, but if your tutor discovers a clear-cut (-and-paste!) case of plagiarism, it may be forwarded to an academic standards committee who will make a decision based on the evidence presented. This might also involve a 'hearing' at a committee to discuss your case. The penalties, if you're found guilty, will depend on the seriousness of the case, but may include:

- Resubmitting the assignment and, assuming you pass, your mark may be capped at the minimum pass mark or even 0% – which won't do much for your averages, or your reputation.

- In really serious cases where there has been a clear intention to deceive, for example, purchasing a 'bespoke' assignment from an essay-writing service and submitting it, or parts of it, as your own work, you may be asked to leave your course.

Table 11.1 Possible sanctions for plagiarism according to survey of teachers at different institutions (adapted from Glendinning, 2013)

Sanction	% Teachers
Zero mark for the work	85%
Fail the module or subject	57%
Repeat the module or subject	55%
Formal warning letter	55%
Request to rewrite it properly	45%
Verbal warning	38%
Fail the whole programme or degree	25%
Repeat the whole year of study	19%
Suspended from the institution	19%
No action would be taken	4%
Expelled from the institution	2%
Other	17%

One of the reviewers for this book added that there was a case at his university of a student whose degree was rescinded because he was found to have plagiarised, two years after he had graduated; another student apparently handed in an essay with the eBay logo still on the page!

For a report into plagiarism policies in the UK, Irene Glendinning (2013) asked teachers 'What would happen if a student at your institution was found guilty of plagiarism in their assignment?' The responses in Table 11.1 show a range of sanctions. Additional feedback from teachers showed a tendency to be supportive rather than punitive when there was doubt; for example, for 'minor errors', just requiring the student to rewrite their work properly (p. 7).

Tip 92: Don't be an accidental plagiarist

The report into plagiarism policies referred to above also asked teachers and students 'What leads students to decide to plagiarise?' From Table 11.2 we can see that ease of cutting and pasting from the internet, not understanding how to cite and reference, pressures of workload, and weak writing skills featured high on the list (although it is interesting to note that many teachers took a more cynical view: 'they think they will not get caught'!).

While some students resort to plagiarism because they haven't done the work, for others it may be that they simply weren't aware that they *were* plagiarising:

> I sit on some disciplinaries for students who have been accused of plagiarism and the two types of students that I see are those that panic and have not done the work, and plagiarise in order just to submit the work on time, and those who genuinely do not understand that they have plagiarised. It can be as simple as not referencing or not putting things in quotation marks; that counts as plagiarism ... (Innovation, Universities, Science and Skills Committee, 2009: 123–124)

So make sure you are clear about what plagiarism is and how to avoid it. After reading this chapter you should have a pretty good idea. And if you are panicking because the deadline is looming and you haven't done the work, go and see your tutor and perhaps you may be able to negotiate an extension (if there's good reason). Plagiarism is cheating, and if you get caught you could lose out on getting your degree. It's not worth it.

Table 11.2 Reasons students plagiarise: student and teacher questionnaires

Reasons students plagiarise	Students	Teachers
It is easy to cut and paste from the internet	52%	77%
They don't understand how to cite and reference	35%	62%
They are unable to cope with the workload	33%	43%
They think their written work is not good enough	31%	42%

(Continued)

Table 11.2   (Continued)

Reasons students plagiarise	Students	Teachers
Their reading comprehension skills are weak	30%	47%
They can't express another person's ideas in their own words	28%	66%
They feel external pressure to succeed	28%	2%
They have always written like that	28%	45%
They feel the task is completely beyond their ability	27%	13%
Assignments tasks are too difficult or not understood	26%	9%
They are not aware of penalties	23%	13%
They run out of time	22%	77%
Unclear criteria and expectations for assignments	22%	8%
They think they will not get caught	17%	87%
Plagiarism is not seen as wrong	17%	49%
They don't want to learn anything, just pass the assignment	16%	43%
There is no teacher control on plagiarism	8%	2%
They think the lecturer will not care	7%	17%
They don't see the difference between group work and collusion	7%	42%
Other	6%	2%

summary

For many students new to university the 'P' word creates anxiety and uncertainty about when to cite your sources, and what precisely will result in a charge of plagiarism. This chapter has clarified the boundaries, but if you are in any doubt make sure you acknowledge your sources.

12

How not to present graphs and charts

In the survey of tutors, problems with tables and figures were relatively low down the list as a source of marker distress, but this presumably reflects the fact that they don't feature in all assignments, particularly essays. When they do feature, however, there are two common problems which were highlighted in the survey:

What tutors dislike

- Tables and figures not numbered or discussed
- Tables and figures that appear from nowhere - without introduction and, worse, sometimes without any explanation

In this chapter we'll take a brief look at these two issues before seeing what not to do with graphs. Finally, we'll look at some tips on how to mislead with statistics.

Tip 93: Always number and title your tables/figures

No matter how many times I emphasise this, there are always a few students who fail to provide a number and title for their tables and figures, or provide a description instead of a title. For example:

Table 1: Bar chart comparing age for male and female students ✓ ☺

not:

Table 1 showing females are much older than male students ✗ ☹

Tip 94: Always introduce and explain your tables/figures

Another common problem is when a table or a figure suddenly appears in the text without any warning, and you wonder 'what's this got to do with anything?' So always introduce tables and figures in the text before they appear. For example, you might write, 'As we can see from Table 1, ...' or 'Figure 1 illustrates ...'.

It's also important, of course, to discuss any information provided in tables and figures – to guide the reader through them, highlighting what's important or relevant. Don't just expect the marker to work it out. Tables and figures should be an additional source of information – they should not be seen as a substitute for detailed discussion in the text.

How *not* to present graphs/charts - a rogue's gallery

The following examples are taken from actual assignments that I have had the pleasure to mark (also cited in Greasley, 2008). I've presented them exactly as they appeared in the assignments. Can you identify the problems?

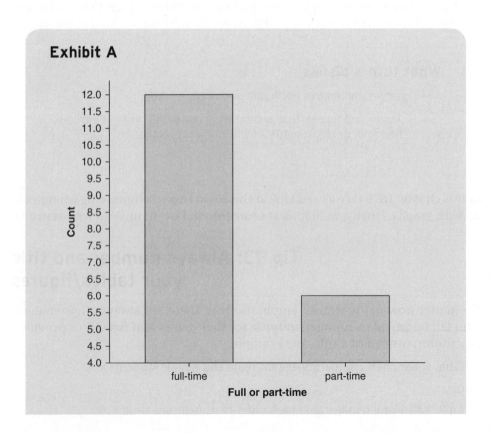

What's wrong with Exhibit A?

Well, first, it's very deceptive. If the purpose of a chart is to provide a visual representation of the results that accurately reflects the data at a glance, then this chart is not the finest of examples. It shows the number of full-time and part-time students on a course. If we were to just glance at the two bars it would appear that there are at least three times as many full-time students as there are part-time. But if you look at the y-axis, you will see that there are actually only twice as many: 6 part-time and 12 full-time. The problem here is that the y-axis starts at 4. There are two further problems:

1   The y-axis increments – can we have half a student?

2   There is no title, e.g. 'Figure 1: Number of students who are full-time and part-time'.

Exhibit B

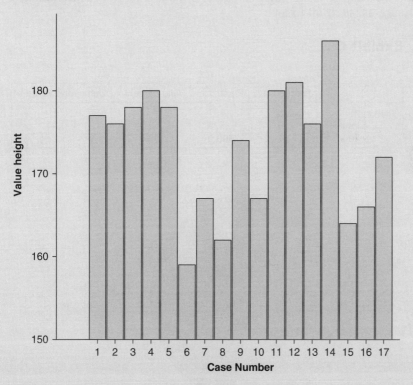

What's wrong with Exhibit B?

There are many things wrong with this chart:

1   There is no title or number (e.g. 'Figure 1: Bar chart showing the height of each student in the class, in no particular order').

(Continued)

(Continued)

2   The *y*-axis (height) has no label of the actual measurements (centimetres).

3   The *y*-axis starts at 150 cm. Is case 14 really three times taller than case 6?

4   If it was really necessary to produce a graph of each individual's height, they might at least have been ordered from lowest to highest.

It's worth noting that these graphs were all produced by the SPSS computer package. Having entered the data, it is very easy to produce graphs by simply clicking on the type of graph you want. The problem is that some students think it is sufficient to simply paste the 'raw output' into their assignments. This is rarely the case, as these examples illustrate, which is why there is a 'chart editor' to edit how they are presented. (This also applies to other computer programs which produce graphs – such as Microsoft Excel.)

Exhibit C

sex

		Frequency	Percent	Valid Percent	Cumulative Percent
Valid	male	8	47.1	47.1	47.1
	female	9	52.9	52.9	100.0
	Total	17	100.0	100.0	

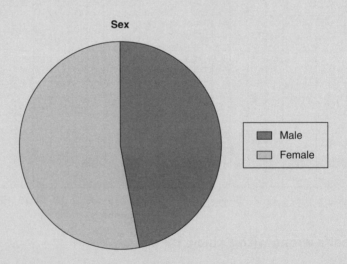

Sex

What's wrong with Exhibit C?

Aside from the fact that neither a table nor a chart is really necessary to illustrate these data – there were eight males and nine females, for goodness' sake – there are a number of other problems:

1   Neither the table nor pie chart have titles.

2   Is the pie chart really necessary to illustrate the table?

3   The pie chart uses shading rather than pattern: since most reports are published in black and white, it's better to use a pattern so that the different elements can be distinguished more easily.

4   There are no numbers and percentages with the pie chart (although the table does provide these).

Exhibit D

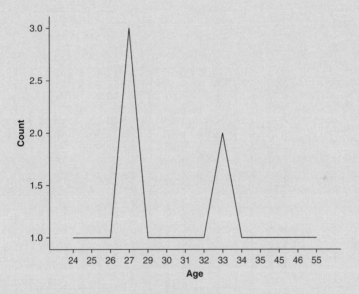

What's wrong with Exhibit D?

This graph has been used to demonstrate the age range of a group of students. There are a few problems:

1   It's a line graph. You would normally select a line graph to represent continuous data which changes over time, e.g. monthly temperature. A line graph is inappropriate in this instance because it has been used to represent distinct age categories – thus producing the ridiculous peak rising from 26 years to 27 years and back down again to 29 years.

2   For some reason the y-axis is at 0.5 intervals – there are no half-people!

(Continued)

(Continued)

3   The chart has no title.

4   It is questionable whether a graph is needed to illustrate ages of individuals within a sample.

Exhibit E

Full/Part-time status
   This bar graph illustrates the frequency distribution of full/part-time status
   N=1 (6%) respondents study part time
   N=16 (94%) respondents study full time

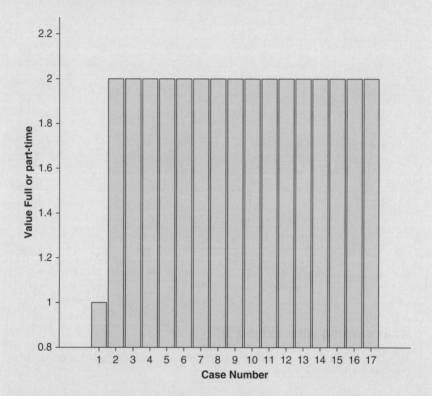

What's wrong with Exhibit E?

This is probably the worst figure I've ever seen (but also the funniest). Aside from the pointless graphical representation, look at the scale.

   If you don't quite understand this figure (and you shouldn't), it might help to know that the student has coded respondents who study part-time as '1' and those who study full-time as '2'.

How to mislead with statistics

In 2005 the US Cable News Network (CNN) presented the results of a poll of 900 people which asked if they agreed with removing the feeding tube from a woman who had been in a 'persistent vegetative state' for several years. As you can see from Figure 12.1, when the results were ordered in terms of political affiliation, Democrats clearly outnumbered Republicans and Independents in their agreement.

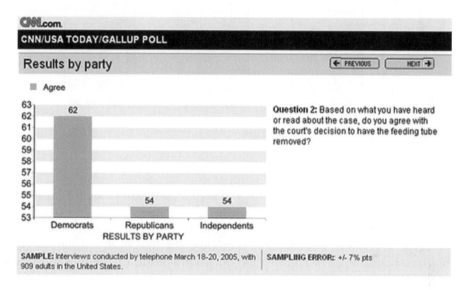

Figure 12.1 CNN poll

Now hopefully you've spotted the problem in Figure 12.1? It's the same trick that was used in Exhibit A: the baseline does not begin at zero. So, although it looks like there was a large difference between Democrats and the other two groups, it was actually quite small: 8%. Figure 12.2 provides a more accurate representation where we can see that the majority of people from each party agreed with removing the feeding tube, but it was slightly higher among Democrats.

There is another important point to note here: the 'sampling error'. If the survey was to be run again with another 900 people, there would probably be a different outcome. This difference has been calculated at ±7% points (noted on the bottom right in Figure 12.1). This means that if the survey was to be run many times over, then the results would probably show 55–69% Democrats who agree and 47–61% Republicans and Independents who agree. And so we can now see that the range of agreement between Democrats, Republicans and Independents overlaps: there is no conclusive difference between them. So it's important to remember that surveys like this produce estimates with a margin of error, and where the 'sampling error' overlaps, as in this case, the results are inconclusive.

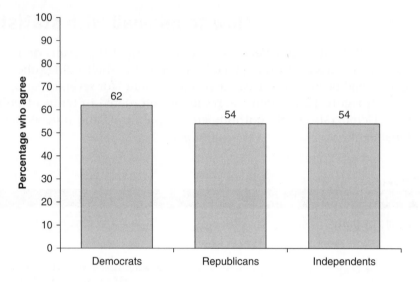

Figure 12.2 CNN poll with zero baseline

Fiddling about with the baseline of graphs is a common tactic for misleading the public. Would you like to invest in my new business? It's doing rather well. Take a look at the profits for 2009 in Figure 12.3 – pretty impressive, I think you'll agree. Of course, I could have presented the figures in a different graph with a zero baseline, as in Figure 12.4, but that wouldn't have looked quite as impressive.

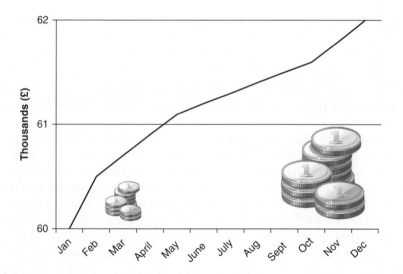

Figure 12.3 Profits for 2009 (impressive!)

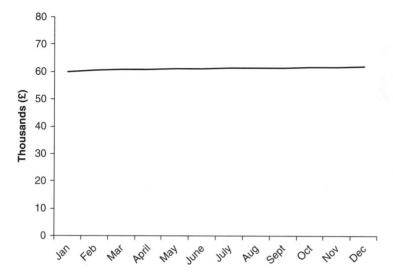

Figure 12.4   Profits for 2009 (unimpressive)

Notice also my inclusion of the coins graphic in Figure 12.3 to illustrate how much profits increased over the year. This is another clever trick to give a false impression – in this case, that profits increased dramatically.

  If you would like more tips on how to mislead using statistics, Darrell Huff (1973) provides many examples in his book *How to Lie with Statistics*; there is also an article in the journal *The American Statistician* by Howard Wainer (1984) called 'How to display data badly'. And for advice on how best to present data in graphs and other visual displays, Edward D. Tufte's (1983) *The Visual Display of Quantitative Information* is one of the classic texts.

summary

If you are going to include any figures, graphs, charts in your assignment, make sure they are:

- numbered with a title
- introduced and discussed in the text
- necessary in the first place - that they have a clear purpose to illustrate or compare data
- an accurate (rather than false or misleading) representation of the data
- edited to ensure that the labelling and axes are appropriate.

13

Presenting your assignment: first impressions count

When the tutor takes your assignment from the pile of marking s/he will gain some important first impressions just by looking at it. Does it appear well presented? Generally speaking, an assignment that is well presented will tend to indicate a good piece of work. This is not always the case, but often the two go together: a student who has put time and effort into the presentation of the assignment will usually have put time and effort into the content (and vice versa). As the following comments indicate, these first impressions may have a powerful effect on the marker:

> [Although] academics might wish to believe that it is the quality of thinking that is assessed in student work ... work which is well presented will stand a better chance of being awarded a higher mark. (Kangis, 2001: 199)

> you signal to the reader the quality of your thinking by the quality of your presentation. (Peck and Coyle, 1999: 122)

> a neat and orderly page has a subliminal effect on the reader, predisposing him to think that the organisation which produced it is likewise neat and orderly and therefore reliable. (Sussams, 1991: 37)

> If it looks awful, it probably is awful. (Greasley, personal observation, 2010)

It's not surprising, then, that problems with presentation were the third most commonly reported source of frustration in the survey of tutors. They included:

- 'Challenging binders' (making it difficult to access and read the assignment)
- Failing to complete the submission/front sheet properly

- Not following guidelines for presentation and word limits:
  - not specifying the word count (or not keeping to it)
  - assignments without page numbers
  - fonts (illegible/too small)
  - single spacing (rather than 1.5 or double spacing)
  - lack of margins
  - poor quality printing
- Lack of proofreading

Tip 95: Avoid challenging binders

First things first, then: make sure your assignment is easy to access and read. There's nothing worse for a marker than having to fumble about trying to access your work. It shouldn't affect the mark of course, but it won't help their mood if they have to struggle to read it and make comments – especially after a long day of marking.

What tutors dislike

- Poor binders that make it difficult to read
- Strange binding practices
- Assignments submitted with each sheet in a separate plastic envelope [this was listed by a few tutors - the problem being that they have to pull each sheet out of the plastic envelope to write comments]

What tutors like

- Assignments presented in secure folders
- Assignments presented in the right size folders!
- Folders where I can turn the pages over easily
- Putting the pages together in a way so that they don't all fall apart when you try to read them

My own pet hate is those narrow plastic spines, especially when the student has tried to cram in twice as many pages as it was designed to hold, so it's packed like a tightly coiled spring waiting to burst out. You can't (daren't) turn the pages over properly, you can't lay it flat to read, and if the left margin is too small you can't see the first word of each line by the time you get to the third page. And then when you do attempt to see the first word of each line, it all comes apart from the spine and you have to spend half an hour trying to get the pages back in.

Tip 96: Complete the submission sheet properly

You'd be surprised how often students fail to complete all the information on the assignment submission sheet. It may not be the most important thing about an assignment, but remember that this is the first sight of your assignment a tutor has – and an incomplete front sheet does not bode well. In fact it's a bit like Sherlock Holmes's deductive reasoning:

Watson: What do you deduce from the fact that they've not completed the front sheet properly, Holmes?

Holmes: That this assignment is going to be problematic, Watson, and will probably receive a poor mark: the lack of attention to detail and inability to follow the guidelines for the front sheet imply that this will be the case for the rest of the assignment.

As the following comments from the survey reveal, common problems include: failing to spell the module leader's name correctly, putting down the wrong module leader or even the wrong module (a good first impression?)

What tutors dislike

- Spelling my name wrong on the front sheet. I have had a least six variations of [my name]
- Putting the wrong module leader's name
- Putting the wrong module name down
- Not knowing what programme they are registered on!
- Missing information on the front sheet – if they can't be bothered to complete the front sheet properly, what does that say about the rest of it?!

Tip 97: Keep to the word count

What tutors dislike

- Not adhering to the word limit!
- Going over the word count, but pretending that it is within the specified limit by putting this on their front sheet!

- Missing word counts – why might this be?
- Text in boxes for no apparent reason other than to avoid being in the word count

It's often tempting for students to stray beyond the word count in pursuit of higher marks. This is a risky strategy with potentially punitive consequences. The University of Bradford (2016), for example, has strict guidelines regarding assignment word limits:

> Assessed work which exceeds a specified maximum permitted length will be subject to a penalty deduction of marks equivalent to the percentage of additional words over the limit. The limit excludes bibliographies, diagrams and tables, footnotes, tables of contents and appendices of data.

So, if it's a 2,000-word assignment and you've written 2,200 words, this could have a serious impact, reducing the mark by 10%.

What's all this fuss over a few extra words, you may ask? Well, word limits are there to:

- standardise the length of the assignment to make it fair for all students (it's unfair if you go well beyond the word count in an attempt to gain an advantage)
- provide a guide to the detail and depth required
- force you to focus on the most important and relevant areas for discussion

This last point is particularly important since it means that you have to be selective and prioritise the information that you will be including in your assignment. So if you do find that you're over the word limit, there are two things you can do:

1. Edit and rephrase your text to make the wording more concise. I gave an example of this in Chapter 9 (Box 9.1) where I managed to cut the number of words in a paragraph by half (from 95 words to 41 words).

2. Remove or reduce the length of those passages and sections in your assignment which are not making an important contribution to the argument and the case you are making (usually the more descriptive sections).

Students adopt some interesting strategies to get round the word limit – for example, by putting text into boxes or appendices. You might get away with one or two boxes, if appropriate, but you really should avoid dumping important information in appendices for the reasons discussed earlier (Tip 33).

It's also quite amusing when students ask if it has to be exactly the number of words specified. It doesn't, of course, and the idea of going away to add some words for the sake of it (any words?) is frankly perplexing. Box 13.1 provides some dubious advice from students about the need to observe word limits.

box 13.1

Keeping to the word limit: advice from other students

On a website called thestudentroom.co.uk, the following query was posted:

If the word limit for an essay is 3000 and i go over by 80 words is that ok?

They don't count (not unless they're REALLY nerdy) ... 80 extras in a 3000 word essay is small potatoes, I'm sure you'll be able to sneak 'em through. But if you're that worried, surely it's possible to take just 80 words out?

So ... do they sit there and count the words? It won't look any different to 3000 with just 80 extra words.

totally depends on the lecturer ... normally 10% is ok, but some are v.strict. 80 words they won't notice, just lie on the word count!

Source: www.thestudentroom.co.uk/showthread.php?t=269376 (accessed August 2009)

Tip 98: Follow the guidelines for formatting and presentation

What markers like

- Paying careful attention to guidelines for the assignment and presentation of work – these are easy marks to gain
- That the student has managed to follow the guidelines in terms of presentation
- Having read and followed handbook guidance on format, referencing, etc.

What markers dislike

- Small/illegible fonts
- Assignments with no page numbers
- A mixture of font types, sizes and spacing!
- Text not double-spaced (if requested; not following guidelines again!)
- Poor quality printing
- 'Lonely headings' – those that appear at the foot of the page with the relevant text appearing on the next page

There should be a list of guidelines for formatting and general presentation of your assignment, and this should generally include the following specifications:

- Font type and size: use fonts that are easy to read (usually Arial or Times New Roman, and usually 12 point size)

- Line spacing: usually at least 1.5 spacing

- Margins: usually at least 3 cm left and right (so there's room for any binding on the left and comments on the right)

- Page numbers: in case the pages get mixed up, but also in case the marker wants to point out something on a particular page

- Print quality: a poor print quality does not give a good impression

You should adhere to the guidelines and show that you've put some effort into the presentation. As the comments cited at the beginning of this chapter illustrate, poor presentation may have a greater influence than you, or indeed your marker, realise.

Tip 99: **Think about 'white space'**

White space is empty space on the page, for example, around the margins and between the paragraphs. People like 'white space'. It's easier on the eye and looks less daunting than a page packed with dense text and no paragraphs.

If you put some thought into the look of your page, this will give your assignment a more professional appearance. I've provided two examples of how white space may be used in Figure 13.1. Which do you think looks better? Think about the impression your tutor will gain when s/he picks up your assignment and flicks through the pages.

Tip 100: **Proofread your assignment**

This tip would have been equally at home in Chapter 9, but I've included it here because it should be one of the last things you do.

What markers like

- Evidence that time has been taken to proofread the essay and ensure there are no typos, etc.

- Careful attention being paid to structure and flow of an assignment which demonstrates drafting and proofreading have been done

- Close attention to detail re spelling, referencing, etc.

- Signs that it may have been read prior to submission(!)

Left panel:

Inconsistent use of 'white space' on the page gives a poor impression. This paragraph starts a fair way down the page for some reason and we have bullet points inconsistently spaced:

• Bullet point one
• Bullet point two

• Bullet point three

Then we have a paragraph starting with no line space after the bullets.

Now we have a new paragraph with lots of white space above it for some reason – and it uses a different font.

It would also have looked more professional if there were larger margins at either side and the text was justified (though this may depend on preferences and guidelines).

It also doesn't help matters when a heading appears at the foot of the page – try to ensure that headings always have a least one line of text underneath them.

Lonely Heading

Right panel:

This looks much better. Consistent use of 'white space' and spacing on the page. There's also a header on each page providing the student's ID number which not only looks good but is useful in case the pages come loose and get detached.

• Bullet point one
• Bullet point two
• Bullet point three

Notice also that the margins have been increased – which is not only important for how it looks but also provides space for the tutor to add comments.

I've also moved the page number from the top right of the page to the bottom centre and added a line separating the footer and the header above. Nice.

The lonely heading has also been removed – better to have a bit of white space at the bottom than a heading with no text. Overall then, hopefully you can see the importance of paying attention to the presentation – consistent use of white space, fonts, line spacing, and margins. It looks more professional and gives a much better first impression.

Figure 13.1 Thinking about 'white space': which assignment looks better?

In Chapter 1, I proposed an analogy between marking assignments and going out for a ride in the car: a well-written and structured assignment provides a smooth, clear run for the marker, whereas a poorly written assignment is like travelling along a bumpy road and having to stop every few seconds because the traffic lights turn red. This is what it's like when an assignment contains lots of grammatical and spelling mistakes and you find yourself stumbling over every other sentence. Needless to say, this may have an impact on the marker's mood, and the mark.

So always take the time to proofread your assignment four tie pin miss takes, spelling errors, and incomplete sentences. A few minor miss steaks may bee forgivable, butt if they stared to mound up that will affect yore mark. Try to get a fiend to proofread your assignment if you can, since they often fined many problems witch you will knot to notice. And don't rely on the spell-checker. It didn't highlight any of these mistakes and it fails to highlight incomplete.

Tip 101: Give your assignment a title

The title may be the assignment question, but if you are asked to choose your own topic, don't forget to include a title that reflects the topic you have chosen – so that the marker will know immediately what s/he has to look forward to.

summary

In this chapter we have seen the importance of following guidelines and paying attention to how your work is presented. First impressions count, and that's because, usually, 'one instance shows the rest' (as was discussed in chapter 6). So always try to complete your assignment with time to spare before submission to allow for final checks and proofreading. And definitely don't submit at the last minute and go down a grade (Tip 13).

14

Feedback and feed-forward

Imagine that you've been asked to cook a fancy meal for a celebrity chef who will be judging the results. You have a selection of ingredients from which to choose and one hour to prepare the meal. When you present the meal to the chef for his judgement, he looks at it, frowns, and says you should have put more thought into the presentation ('we eat with our eyes'); he then complains about the combination of ingredients you've chosen (they just don't work together); and when he finally tastes it, he informs you that the fish is overcooked and the vegetables are undercooked. All in all, it's a fair effort, mate, but there's room for improvement.

Now imagine that the chef actually guides you through the process, advising as you select and prepare the ingredients, season and cook them, and present it all on the plate so it looks good. With a little bit of guidance during the process, you are much more likely to produce a better meal. This is because in the first instance you only had 'summative feedback', after the meal had been completed, whereas in the second case you had 'formative feedback', when it was not too late to influence the outcome.

Tip 102: Get some formative feedback

On many courses there will be the opportunity to obtain formative feedback on a plan of your assignment prior to submission. If this is available, my advice is to take up the offer, especially if you're not clear about what is expected in your assignment or if you're particularly concerned about achieving a high mark and 'ticking all the boxes' (so to speak). The cue-seekers (discussed in Chapter 3) will usually avail themselves of this opportunity (whether it's advertised or not).

On some courses there may also be the opportunity to obtain formative feedback on a draft of your assignment (some will even give you a mark and say what you need to do to increase it for the final submission). The problem is, of course, that you need to be very well organised in order to complete a draft, pass it on to your tutor, wait for the comments, and revise your final version, all before the submission date. And remember, if you are sending a draft by email, it may be some time before your tutor has the chance to look at it:

Student: Have you read my assignment?

Tutor: No, when did you send it?

Student: Last night

Tutor: Hmm...

It's also important to be aware that if you do submit a draft to your tutor for comments, you may be letting yourself in for a lot of extra work revising it. However, it should be worthwhile because you will be receiving specific suggestions for improvements from the person who will be marking your assignment. Have a look at the list of comments I made on one draft assignment in Box 14.1 and think about the difference they might have made to the grade. For some students, the prospect of receiving an extensive list of comments like those in Box 14.1 might be the biggest deterrent to submitting a draft of their assignment, because of the extra work. You can ignore the feedback, of course, but bear in mind that one of the complaints in the survey of tutors was 'Ignoring feedback given when a draft assignment was submitted'.

box 14.1

Formative feedback on a draft assignment

Obtaining formative feedback from your tutor on a draft assignment can provide some important suggestions to improve your assignment. For example, here's a list of suggestions I noted on one draft assignment:

Title

Suggested giving the assignment a specific title for the topic chosen

Introduction

Suggested expanding the introduction to provide a brief outline of the topics covered in the assignment and what is concluded

Referencing

Noted some issues with references and referencing, e.g. where needed to add references for claims/statistics/source of figures; errors citing references in the text and quotations without page numbers

(Continued)

(Continued)

Language

Suggested using the impersonal voice rather than 'the author'

Noted a couple of unclear sentences which needed a little more explanation to clarify a point

Tables and Figures

Pointed out need to introduce figures in the text (two figures suddenly appeared vaguely related to a preceding discussion – but they should have been specifically referred to in the text)

Suggested a brief comparison of the two figures highlighting key differences

Structure

Suggested an additional section of relevant material, a subheading where discussion drifted into new topic, and some refocusing of assignment

Content and Discussion

Advised against overuse of lists (lapsing into lists) and bullet points in place of discussion and reflective comments (it's discussion that gets marks), and suggested some of the lists could go in an appendix

Suggested need for more discussion and critical reflection about the issues outlined (and not to leave critical reflections until the conclusion)

Tip 103: Read the feedback

A common complaint among university tutors is that many students don't read and reflect upon the feedback that comes with their assignments – they are only interested in the mark. As one tutor complained recently in *Times Higher Education*:

> I bang on about these problems [grammar, punctuation, etc.] on every essay feedback sheet, but here's the thing: students do not read them.

> I recently asked several classes of students, including an academic writing group where discussion of this sort is part of the course, about whether such criticisms are noted. They said that the vast majority never read the comments – they just wanted to know the mark. How's that for dispiriting? (Dann, 2009)

These concerns about ignoring feedback were also highlighted in the survey of tutors.

What tutors dislike

- Ignoring feedback given when a draft assignment was submitted
- Not learning from the feedback given to previous assignments or to comments on the draft assignment

What tutors like

- Clearly engaging with feedback from previous assignments and using this to build upon skills
- Evidence of having taken notice of feedback on previous assignments and correcting errors

Now the quality and quantity of feedback you get from tutors may vary, but it should highlight key issues to address in order to avoid repeating the same mistakes, as well as what you need to do to improve future assignments, so it's important to reflect on the comments and *think about what you need to do next time* (and if there's anything you're not clear about, or disagree with, make an appointment to see the tutor so you can discuss the feedback). When Quinton and Smallbone (2010) asked a group of second- and third-year students to reflect on feedback from previous assignments and note what they needed to do in future, these were the most common issues to address:

- check marking criteria
- improve referencing
- read around subject more
- provide more evidence
- extend ideas
- better explanation of ideas
- give clearer structure
- make more of a plan for my essay
- apply more theory
- be more analytical
- move from being descriptive to analysing
- improve time management
- start assignment earlier
- leave time to review the assignment once written

Does that sound familiar?

Tip 104: **Get some feed-forward**

Finally, why don't you ask for some assignment tips? You've already had a bucketful of tips from this book, but there will most likely be some specific tips that are relevant to each particular assignment. Assuming your tutor has set the same or similar assignment for a previous cohort, he should have an idea of the common problems that cropped up. What were they? There's an example of this in Box 14.2. It's known as 'feed-forward': taking stock of the issues raised in previous assignments and feeding it forward to the next group of students.

box   14.2

Feed-forward from tutors' comments on mark sheets

When Duncan (2007: 274) and colleagues were looking to feed-forward advice to students based on comments from past mark sheets, they came up with a list of issues similar to those in the survey of tutors. They are presented below:

Feed-forward issues*

Use more of the relevant literature

Use more references

Proofread

Improve organisation and structure

Improve/correct punctuation

Check and improve spelling and grammar

Avoid over-clever language

Give more detail

Use more specific/practical examples

Support your points by reference or logical argument

Use academic style

Focus on the question and cover all key points

Deepen analysis of key issues

Sharpen critique

Identify and develop implications

Link theory and practice

*Based on the analysis of 150 mark sheets from the work of 16 students.

But if you'd rather ignore all the tips and advice in this book, try completing the alternative assignment checklist in Table 14.1 to see how many marks you *could* lose.

Table 14.1   How to reduce your mark: an assignment checklist

The following form should be completed prior to submission of your assignment by entering a tick ✓ for each statement. If you do need to enter an × next to any statement please return to your assignment and make the necessary revisions.

Alternative Assignment Checklist	Yes ✓	No ×

Presenting your work

1   I have used a binder that will make it difficult for you to access and read my assignment

2   I have not completed all the details on the submission sheet

3   I have not kept to the word count

4   I have not included the word count

5   I have used single line spacing to make it more difficult for you to add your sarcastic comments

6   I have used a mixture of font sizes and line spacing in parts for no apparent reason

7   I have tried to ensure that at least one of my headings prints out at the foot of the page with no text underneath it (i.e. a 'lonely heading' with the relevant text starting on the next page)

8   I know there are guidelines about how to present my assignment, and I'm sure they are very interesting, but I prefer my own particular style which is different from all the rest

Answering the question

9   I have not included the question at the beginning of the assignment because I've got a rough idea of what it's supposed to be about

10   I have used an abridged version of the title, focusing on the bits I'm interested in

11   I have spent most of the essay describing the issue in question (only relevant for essays with 'criticise' or 'evaluate' in the title)

12   While I found the question that you set quite intriguing, I decided to write about what I'm interested in because it was so much easier

Marking criteria

13   I have not consulted the marking criteria that you will be using to mark my assignment (because that would mean I'd really need to think about how I'm going to address it)

(Continued)

Table 14.1 (Continued)

	Yes ✓	No ×
Alternative Assignment Checklist		

Introducing the assignment

14   I have assumed you know what I am talking about so I haven't bothered with an introduction outlining my topic, aims, etc.

Structuring the assignment and following guidelines

15   I have avoided using headings and subheadings to structure the assignment because they may have interrupted my stream of consciousness

16   I have used my initiative and changed the focus and order of the assignment to suit myself (only relevant where strict guidelines are issued by the tutor)

Language: writing style, clarity and detail

17   I have assumed you have a good grasp of my particular topic to save time explaining things properly

18   I have included some obscure abbreviations and acronyms without explaining what they mean

19   I have provided clarification for the meaning of an abbreviation or acronym but not until the third occasion of its use in the text

20   I have made vague, general references to important information without specifying the details in order to give my work a sense of mystery and intrigue

21   I have talked about everything in general but nothing in particular, avoiding the use of examples to illustrate any points

22   I have used words and expressions (e.g. 'it is for the achievement of this necessity') that would make me sound a bit odd if I used them in actual conversation

23   I have included some obscure words in long and complicated sentences to show that I've been suffering from complex thoughts that are impossible to express clearly

24   I just couldn't face proofreading it

25   I haven't bothered spell-checking it either in order to provide you with some 'amusing' mistakes

Plagiarism

26   When I have found relevant information in a textbook, or on the internet, I have simply copied it rather than using my own words (and without a reference, for obvious reasons)

27   I did actually buy a 'similar' assignment from essaysrus.com, but even though I gave them the assignment brief and then requested a few changes, I just used it as a guide because I was a bit busy

Alternative Assignment Checklist	**Yes** ✓	**No** ×

Concluding the assignment

28   I have not included a conclusion summarising my assignment and my position on the issues because it's difficult to know what to make of it, having just read through it

References and referencing

29   I did my references in a rush at the end to avoid getting bogged down in the tedious chore of checking they're all present and correct

30   I ignored key references that were referred to in the course in favour of my own, mainly electronic, sources

31   Where I have not been able to locate the details of a particular reference, I have included what I can remember

32   In order to make a good impression I have added a long list of references, most of which weren't cited in the text

33   I have pasted in references from a previous assignment, so some of them may not actually be relevant to this particular assignment

34   I have not checked exactly how I'm supposed to cite references in the text, but I do know brackets appear somewhere in all this

35   Where possible I have used obscure internet references rather than those boring, peer-reviewed journals you keep banging on about

36   I have made numerous statements derived from the findings of studies (e.g. effectiveness of treatments) while managing to avoid revealing the source of these claims

Appendices

37   I have put lots of stuff in the appendix that I couldn't be bothered integrating into the main text. It's kind of relevant, but I'll leave that for you to work out

38   There are some things in the appendices that I've not referred to in the main text, so you'll have a nice surprise when you get to the end of my assignment

Tables and figures

39   I have not introduced tables and figures in the text before they occur so you can wonder why they have suddenly appeared and what relevance they have to anything you have been reading

40   Where possible, I have tried to organise it so that my tables and figures continue over on to the next page

41   I have not numbered tables or figures or given them titles since this should be obvious from the text

(Continued)

Table 14.1 (Continued)

	Yes ✓	No ×
Alternative Assignment Checklist		

Self-assessment forms

42	I have completed the self-assessment form, listing all the things I know I should have done but didn't

Getting advice

43	Although I really didn't have a clue what I was supposed to be doing in this assignment, I carried on regardless without seeking any advice
44	I am looking forward to seeing you during the summer break to discuss my resubmission when all my friends are at Glastonbury

summary

Formative feedback from your tutor is probably the most valuable aspect of teaching you receive at university, because you are receiving individual advice that steers you in the right direction to improve your assignment; make use of it.

15

Writing research/ project reports

Many assignments in the social and health sciences, particularly at postgraduate level, involve writing about research projects, so in this chapter I've provided some tips for writing up research/project reports.

Tip 105: The key criteria for writing up a research report are clarity, detail and structure

The most common problems in my experience of marking research reports are:

- **Lack of clarity**. *You* know what you're talking about and so does the other expert on the topic, who lives in Minnesota, but most other people, including your tutor, may not. In order to achieve *clarity*, you might imagine that you've been asked to produce the report for a professional who knows very little about the subject you are investigating and the research methods you are using. Remember the 'curse of knowledge' (Tip 63).

- **Lack of detail**. In order to achieve the necessary *detail* you might like to imagine that the person reading it could actually conduct the research project based on the detail in your report (this is particularly the case for quantitative research).

- **Structure**. There are established guidelines for structure, which should be adhered to – the subject of the next tip.

Tip 106: Follow the established structure for writing the report

A research report is *not* an essay; it requires a more formal structure to ensure the researcher has addressed the relevant issues with the necessary detail. Typically, it will include the headings provided in Table 15.1. In a research *proposal* (where you're outlining a project that you're intending to do), you might also include an outline of:

- resources required for the project, e.g. materials, software, training

- how the project will be managed (project management), e.g. Gantt charts scheduling activities with timeframes

- how you intend to disseminate the results, e.g. report to stakeholders, presentations, academic articles

Table 15.1 Typical sections for a research report

Section	Contents
Abstract	A concise summary of the report/proposal (200-300 words) providing a brief background and aims of the study, the methods used and sample, outline of analysis and results, conclusions.
Introduction	Background to the study, the problem and how you are addressing it. Review of relevant literature identifying gaps and how your study contributes. Research question; aims and objectives.
Methodology	Including: • Design - methodological approach and design, e.g. quantitative (experiment, questionnaire survey) or qualitative (interviews, focus groups) • Sample - sampling frame (the accessible population from which your sample is drawn) and actual sample • Materials - e.g. questionnaires • Procedure - detailed account of how the research was conducted.
Ethical issues	Discussion of any ethical issues and how addressed.
Data analysis	How you will be analysing the data, e.g. statistical analysis of questionnaires, thematic coding of interviews.
Results	Presentation of results.
Discussion	Discussion of the study with reference to relevant literature and its contribution to the area of interest; limitations.
Conclusion	Summary and recommendations.
References	List of works cited in the report.
Appendices	Materials used, e.g. example of questionnaire, patient information leaflet.

Tip 107: An abstract is an abstract – not a general introduction

An abstract is a brief, concise summary (usually limited to 200–300 words) which gives the reader a quick overview of the study. It is not a general introduction to the topic. Make it the last thing you write – since you need to know what you have said in order to provide the summary. It should provide the following information:

- Brief background to the research

- Purpose/aims of the study

- Methods used and the sample

- Results

- Brief conclusions

I've provided an example in Box 15.1.

box 15.1

Example of an abstract

As an example, I've reproduced the abstract from the journal article upon which this book is based (Greasley and Cassidy, 2010).

When it comes round to marking assignments: how to impress and how to 'distress' lecturers ...

What do lecturers look for when marking essays? What impresses them and what frustrates them? In this paper, we present the results of a survey which asked lecturers to address these questions. Thirty-two lecturers responded to an email survey in which they listed the problems they found most frustrating when marking essays and the factors which most impressed them. This resulted in 206 comments related to sources of frustration and 139 comments listing factors which impress them. The comments were then coded into themes and ranked in order of importance by 16 lecturers from the original sample. The results highlight a range of issues that may be useful for lecturers when discussing assignments, and instructive for students when writing their assignments.

While this might not be the best of abstracts (where's the brief background to the research?), it does provide a relatively succinct overview of the study:

- *Purpose/aims of the study*. What do lecturers look for when marking – what impresses and frustrates them?
- *Methods used and the sample*. An email survey of 32 lecturers (notice that the sample size is actually specified)
- *Results*. Number of comments – coded into themes and ranked
- *Brief conclusions*. Comments highlight a range of issues (perhaps this could have been more specific, listing the main issues)

Tip 108: **Make your aims clear**

The aim should be a general statement outlining the purpose of the study and what you are aiming to accomplish (not *how* it will be accomplished). For example: 'The aim of this study is to compare two therapies in the treatment of...'; or 'The aim of this study is to examine the experiences of patients who...'. The aim may also be stated in terms of a formal research question. For example: 'Is treatment X more effective than treatment Y for condition A?'

If it is an experimental study, you may also need to state your aims in terms of a hypothesis (prediction). For example:

> **Hypothesis:** People asked to hold a pen with their teeth will find cartoons funnier than people who are asked to hold a pen with their lips.

And then you should pose a 'null hypothesis', which assumes there is no difference:

> **Null hypothesis:** Whether people hold a pen in their teeth or their lips will make no difference to their 'funniness ratings' of cartoons.

Statistical analysis will tell you whether to retain or reject the null hypothesis. And since Strack et al. (1988) did find a difference – people asked to hold the pen with their teeth found the cartoons funnier than those who were asked to hold the pen with their lips – we conclude that the null hypothesis was rejected. (Just to clarify, this experiment was designed to investigate the 'facial feedback hypothesis': holding the pen in your lips inhibits smiling, whereas holding the pen in your teeth facilitates smiling. Smile and you'll feel happy.)

Tip 109: **Make your objectives SMART**

Objectives are the steps to achieve the aim – how it will be accomplished. They should be as SMART as possible:

- **S**pecific - clearly defined: what exactly are you intending to do and how?
- **M**easurable - so that you'll know when outcomes have been achieved
- **A**chievable - within the resources available
- **R**ealistic - outcomes can be achieved
- **T**imebound - set within a given timeframe

So, for example, if your objective is stated as 'to look into the benefits of counselling for patients', there's probably some room for improvement, along the following lines:

- Objective 1: To measure the mental health benefits of short-term counselling (6 sessions) for all patients attending the Killingham Health Clinic over a 12-month period using the Hospital Anxiety and Depression Scale administered at referral to the service and 6 months after the final counselling session

- Objective 2: To investigate patient satisfaction with the service using a postal questionnaire to all patients during the 12-month study period and interviews with a sample of patients who respond

- Objective 3: To explore the views of health professionals about the service through a focus group with the counsellors

Failing to present clear and specific objectives is one of the most common pitfalls of projects (see Tip 128: 'projects fail at the start, not at the end'). Hopefully, you'll notice that the objectives listed above try to really spell out the details using the SMART criteria, e.g. it's not just counselling but, more *specifically*, short-term counselling, the *timeframe* for the evaluation is 12 months, and outcomes will be *measured* using the Hospital Anxiety and Depression Scale.

Tip 110: Specify the sample (and the sampling frame)

If you're writing a research proposal, try to be as specific as possible about the sample/participants. The worst thing you can do, and it often happens, is to simply indicate that the sample will be 'small' or 'large'. What is small: 5, 10, 20, 30? What is large: 20 tutors, 1,000 students?

It is also important to contextualise the sample by indicating the 'sampling frame'. This is the accessible population from which your sample is drawn. For example, if you are interviewing 20 students to find out how they felt about a course, how many students actually took the course? If it was 120, how did you select these 20? And are they representative of the total sample?

This also highlights the importance of specifying the sampling method. There are various options, such as:

- Random (probability) sample - where people have an equal chance of being selected (if so, *how* do you ensure it is 'random'? - see below)

- Quota sampling - to ensure relevant categories are equally represented, e.g. males and females

- Convenience sample - e.g. the next 20 patients, referrals over 3 months, a class of students

- Purposive sampling - identifying relevant interviewees for your purposes, e.g. patients with similar experiences

If you've opted for a random sample, it's important to specify *how* the sample was randomised to each condition or treatment, because there's 'random' and there's really 'random'. The problem is that if your sample is not truly randomised, you might be accused of selection bias. For example, if your 'random' selection entails recruiting every other patient to one or other treatment, it could be open to systematic bias from the person recruiting the patients, as the following scenario from Ben Goldacre (2009: 49) illustrates:

Let's imagine there is a patient who the homeopath believes to be a no-hoper, a heart-sink patient who'll never really get better, no matter what treatment he or she gets, and the next place available on the study is for someone going into the 'homeopathy' arm of the trial. It's not inconceivable that the homeopath might just decide – consciously or unconsciously – that this particular patient 'probably wouldn't really be interested' in the trial. But if, on the other hand, this no-hoper patient had come into the clinic at a time when the next place on the trial was for the placebo group, the recruiting clinician might feel a lot more optimistic about signing them up.

In this respect, it's interesting to note that studies have shown that trials with 'dodgy methods of randomisation overestimate treatment effects by 41 per cent' (Goldacre, 2009: 50). So it's partly about bias and partly about trust. Ideally, the recruitment should be conducted blindly and/or by a third person so it's not open to these accusations.

Tip 111: Write the procedure section so that the reader could replicate your study

Try to be very specific and detailed when writing up the method and procedure sections. Ideally, the reader should be able to replicate your study based on the detail you provide in your report. For example, if the study involved a questionnaire, how was it distributed to participants? Was it posted to participants to complete and return, or was it completed in the presence of the researcher? These details may be important. Studies have shown that the way in which a questionnaire is administered – self-completion or in the presence of an interviewer – can influence the responses (Lyons et al., 1999).

For randomised controlled trials in health research, a checklist of criteria has been developed by the CONSORT group (Consolidated Standards of Reporting Trials) in order to promote the transparent reporting of trials (www. consort-statement.org, accessed February 2016).

Tip 112: Note the limitations and make some recommendations

In the discussion section, you should include critical reflections on the study (e.g. design of the questionnaire, relevance of outcome measures, limitations for generalising due to small sample sizes). The conclusion should include general implications of the study and suggestions or recommendations for further research.

Common problems in research reports

In Table 15.2, I've highlighted some common problems from my own experience of marking research reports.

Table 15.2 Typical sections used for reports of research – and some common problems

Section	Common problems
Abstract	• It says it's an abstract but it isn't really; instead it reads more like a general introduction rather than an overview of what's in the report (outlining the methods, sample, results)
Introduction	• Although it is useful to start with the broader context to the topic, sometimes students start too broadly and need to get to the point sooner; that is, the key literature for the topic of the report • Relevant literature and studies are not prioritised for relevance, or critically appraised • Assumes reader is familiar with topic/subject area • Lacks a clear rationale for study (what you expect to find and why) • Aims and research question not clearly spelled out; objectives are not SMART (specific, measurable, achievable, realistic, time-bound)
Methodology	• Not clear enough, not specific enough, not sufficiently detailed (could the reader replicate the study from your account?) • Choice of design/approach not justified (why this approach and not others? What are the advantages and disadvantages?) • Lacks references to research methods literature, e.g. about questionnaire design, interviewing • Doesn't adhere to the recommended structure for reporting methodology (design, sample, procedure etc.) • Sample not specified or justified • Sampling frame not provided (i.e. the accessible population from which the sample is drawn)
Results	• Lacks clarity and critical reference to literature • Not related back to aims and objectives or hypotheses
Discussion	• Not enough reflection • Not related to practice (the 'so what?' factor)
Conclusion	• No recommendations
References	• Not in correct format, etc.
Appendices	• None provided • Too many provided (used as a dumping ground for details that should be in the main text) • Not numbered correctly (difficult to locate)

summary

There is a well-established structure for reporting the results of research, so you should be clear about what each section should contain. In a nut-shell, say what you did, why you did it, how you did it, what you found, and what it means more generally.

16

Doing a systematic literature review

Many students need to do a literature review as part of their assignments or, indeed, as an assignment in itself. This chapter provides some tips on how to conduct a *systematic* literature review, including how to choose an appropriate topic, conduct a systematic search of the literature, and report the results of your search clearly and systematically. The importance of systematic literature reviews is discussed and the need to retain a critical perspective on the accuracy of the academic literature is highlighted – especially since, according to one source referred to later in the chapter, 'most published research findings are false'.

Conducting a systematic literature review

The aim of a systematic literature review is to provide an exhaustive review of the literature on a particular topic. In order to ensure that it has been conducted thoroughly you will need to include details of databases searched, search terms used, and parameters or 'limits' applied (e.g. range of years searched). The key ingredients of a systematic literature review are:

1. Having a clear and specific research question

2. Providing a systematic account of the search process

3. Providing a critical review/appraisal of the literature with new insights - the whole should be greater than the sum of the parts

Tip 113: **Have a clear and specific research question**

The key point here is that the review should not be too broad, otherwise the task will be overwhelming, but not too narrow either. In this respect, consider the following possible topics for a literature review:

A. A systematic review of psychological therapies for anxiety and depression

B. A systematic review of orgone therapy for migraine

C. A systematic review of cognitive behavioural therapy (CBT) for obsessive compulsive disorder

If you're embarking on topic A make sure you allow yourself at least a couple of years to conduct your review as there are numerous psychological therapies used to treat the two most common mental health issues of anxiety and depression. It's too vague, it's too broad and it's too big. Box 16.1 shows how much literature is out there.

Topic B, on the other hand, seems too narrow. The Austrian psychoanalyst Wilhelm Reich discovered orgone energy in the 1930s. He invented the 'orgone accumulator' and the 'orgone shooter' to collect and distribute orgone energy in order to cure all kinds of medical conditions. However, a quick search for 'orgone' on PubMed reveals just 21 articles, most of which are published in journals from the Orgone Institute (some potential for bias there) with just one article discussing headaches (published in 1976). Reich died in Lewisburg Federal Penitentiary where he was serving a two-year term for selling quack medical devices (as well as a machine that draws 'orgone energy' from the atmosphere, causing the formation and dispersion of clouds, known as a Cloudbuster).

Topic C, however, is neither too broad nor too narrow (this is beginning to sound like the three bears): we have a *specific* therapy for a *specific* condition. This should result in a relatively homogenous collection of studies, which can be compared and summarised. The only problem might be that the search retrieves a large number of articles – in which case you might apply some limits to your search (e.g. just quantitative studies looking at outcomes of therapy, or studies in the last 10 years).

box   16.1

Two million articles a year - but who reads them?

Estimates vary, but according to the International Association of Scientific, Technical and Medical Publishers (Ware and Mabe, 2015) there were around 28,000 scholarly peer-reviewed journals in 2012 publishing

(Continued)

(Continued)

around 2.5 million articles a year. The USA is the main source, accounting for 23% of articles, then China (17%), the UK (7%), Japan (6%), Germany (6%) and France (4%). Now you might be wondering who reads all these articles. Well, according some sources, hardly anyone:

> It is a sobering fact that some 90% of papers that have been published in academic journals are never cited. Indeed, as many as 50% of papers are never read by anyone other than their authors, referees and journal editors. We know this thanks to citation analysis, a branch of information science in which researchers study the way articles in a scholarly field are accessed and referenced by others. (Meho, 2007)

These statistics are not, however, substantiated in the article by Meho (and surely it's one thing to read an article and quite another to cite it). When Larivière et al. (2009) examined citations up to five years after an article was published (because you need to allow time for people to read them and produce their own articles) they found that only 12% of papers in medical fields remained uncited, 27% in natural sciences and engineering, and 32% in the social sciences. So the majority of articles do get cited, but not necessarily that much.

Tip 114: **Provide a systematic account of the literature search process**

Having chosen an appropriate topic, the next step is to provide a systematic account of the literature search: terms used, databases searched, number of articles retrieved, and limits applied (if any).

Selecting the appropriate search terms requires careful thought. For example, if you were reviewing the use of CBT for people with learning disabilities then you would need to check the appropriate terminology: in the UK the term 'learning disability' is used, whereas in the USA the preferred term is 'intellectual disability'. Therefore, if you searched using the term 'learning disability' you may miss many articles produced in the USA. Fortunately, many databases have a thesaurus listing the formal standardised terms that you should use to capture relevant articles.

Having selected the appropriate terms, you may need to combine them using Boolean logic (named after the English mathematician George Boole, 1815–1864). This basically means using the terms AND, OR and NOT where, for example:

- cats AND dogs would identify articles where *both* terms are appear in the article (not either)

- cats OR dogs would identify articles where *either* term appears in the article (and so you would retrieve more articles)

- cats NOT dogs would identify articles that do not refer to dogs – if you wanted specifically to exclude dogs

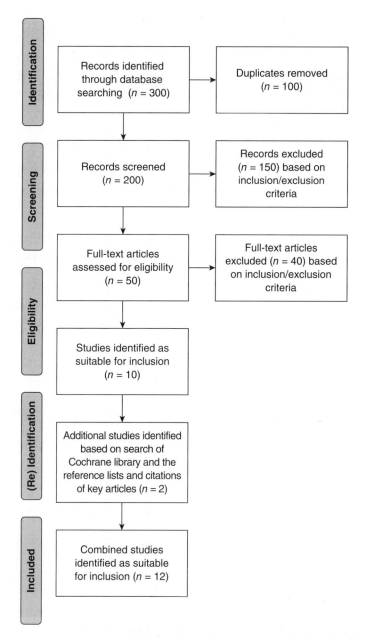

Figure 16.1 Flow diagram of search process

Adapted from PRISMA (Preferred Reporting Items for Systematic Reviews and Meta-Analyses) www.
prisma-statement.org

There are also a few techniques to limit or expand your search:

- Place a phrase in quotes if you want to search using that exact phrase, e.g. "cognitive behavioural therapy" – without the quotes it would retrieve articles with any of the words 'cognitive', 'behavioural' and 'therapy'

- Insert an asterisk after the root stem of a search term to locate various endings, e.g. if you enter psychol* it will locate psychology, psychologist, psychological

- You may also be able to select particular filters provided by the database, e.g. to specify particular types of articles such as 'peer-reviewed'; particular age groups (infants or adults); particular 'populations' (animals or humans); particular 'date ranges' (the last 5 or 10 years)

- You should also be able to limit your search to particular sections of journal articles such as titles or abstracts. This is useful if your search term is likely to retrieve many articles that are not relevant to your research. For example, the term CBT or 'cognitive behavioural therapy' will be used in many articles that are not specifically about CBT, so just searching the titles and/or abstracts should help to limit and focus your search.

It is important to keep a record of the articles retrieved and excluded. This may be done with a flow chart, as illustrated in Figure 16.1. The flow chart provides details of the number of articles found, duplicates removed, abstracts read, items removed in line with the inclusion/exclusion criteria, and any further records found through examining the references from the articles. At the end of the process you will have a selection of relevant studies. This can then be summarised as in Table 16.1.

Table 16.1 Summarising the studies in a table

Authors	Country	Context	Aims of Study	Method	Sample	Main findings	Strengths & limitations
Smith (2010)	England	School	To identify...	Questionnaire	Who and how many	Brief indication of outcomes	
Jones (2008)	USA	Hospital	Etc.				
...							

Do I really need to be so systematic?

Yes, you do. In 1986, double Nobel Prize winner Linus Pauling (1901–1994) published *How to Live Longer and Feel Better* in which he recommended that we all take very large daily doses of vitamin C to prevent the common cold. This recommendation was founded upon Pauling's review of the literature. However, when Paul Knipschild saw Pauling's review he noticed that nearly all the trials Pauling discussed were positive, and there was not much detail about how the search had been conducted; in other words, it did not look like a comprehensive review of the literature. So Knipschild embarked upon his own *systematic* review. He found additional articles, and when only the most credible studies were included in the review, he concluded that vitamin C does not prevent the common cold, although it may decrease its duration and severity.

Pauling had committed the crime of 'cherry picking' – selecting the studies supporting his argument and ignoring those that didn't. He failed to mention five of the top 15 studies in Knipschild's review (Knipschild, 1994).

Tip 115: 'It ain't so much the things we know that gets us into trouble. It's the things we know that ain't so'

We already know from Chapter 8 that critical thinking is one of the most important faculties to develop as an undergraduate, so it should come as no surprise to find out that the literature you are reviewing needs to be critically appraised. The above quotation from Artemus Ward (1834–1867) is particularly relevant in light of a paper written by John Ioannidis in 2005 entitled 'Why most published research findings are false' (which at the time of writing has been cited over 3,000 times, according to Google Scholar). The reasoning behind this claim is that many studies have sample sizes that are too small to draw firm conclusions, and are produced by people who have a vested interest in finding a significant effect. As a result there is a phenomenon known as the 'decline effect', where the magnitude of published discoveries tends to shrink and fade over time as people retest the findings. Thus, according to Ioannidis, of the 49 most highly cited medical papers, only 34 have been retested, and of them 14 had been convincingly shown to be wrong (though still cited). Furthermore, 98% of claims associating genes with disease could not be replicated. For an accessible and interesting overview of 'the decline effect' there is a radio programme on the BBC called *Everything We Know Is Wrong* (BBC iPlayer Radio, 2 September 2014, available at www.bbc.co.uk/programmes/b04f9r4k).

More recently, an initiative to replicate 100 studies from three leading psychology journals reported that key findings from just 39 of the studies could be reproduced (Baker, 2015). Furthermore, where replication was successful, the size of the effect was typically less than half that of the original. For a more detailed discussion of these studies, see Jump (2015).

Critically appraising the studies

Once you have arrived at your selection of articles, it is important to assess their quality in terms of their contribution to the review. There are a few critical appraisal tools that you can use for this. For example, the Critical Appraisal

Skills Programme (CASP) developed by the Public Health Research Unit at the University of Oxford (http://www.casp-uk.net) provides checklists for critically appraising different types of studies, such as randomised controlled trials, systematic reviews and qualitative studies. For example, the checklist for randomised controlled trials includes the questions:

- Was the assignment of patients to treatments randomised? And if so, how was this carried out?

- Was allocation concealed from researchers and patients (double-blind)?

For qualitative studies the checklist includes such questions as:

- Was the recruitment strategy appropriate to the aims of the research and did the authors explain how participants were selected?

- Was the data analysis sufficiently rigorous, e.g. is it clear how themes were derived from the data?

- Is sufficient data presented to support the findings?

- To what extent are contradictory data taken into account?

You might then apply a rating scale to quantify the extent to which these issues are addressed in the articles, e.g. little or no explanation/justification = 1; some explanation/justification = 2; extensive explanation/justification = 3 (see Duggleby et al., 2010). Table 16.2 provides an example. This will allow you to place greater stock in some studies rather than others when writing up the results of your review.

Table 16.2 Quality analysis (extract example. other criteria may apply; see CASP website)

Paper	Clear aims?	Design justified?	Recruitment appropriate?	Data analysis rigorous?	Total
Smith (2010)	3	3	3	3	12
Jones (2008)	1	1	1	1	4

Writing up the review

It is important to bear in mind that the marker is probably not reading your report for enjoyment; s/he will be aiming to extract what s/he needs from your report quickly and efficiently. This means you need to write it very clearly, logically and systematically, using key headings and subheadings:

- Introduction:
  o Outlining the need for your review with reference to the literature
  o Research/review question/aims
- Method:
  o A clear and simple account of the search, including:
    o databases searched
    o key words used
    o limits applied (inclusion/exclusion criteria)
    o outcome of search (with a flow chart showing how you arrived at your articles)
- Results:
  o A summary overview of the studies included (with a table)
  o Critically appraisal studies (with a table)
  o A synthesis of the findings (key themes from reviewing the group of articles)
- Conclusions and recommendations

In this chapter we have discussed what is required to produce a clear and specific research question for your review, as well as a comprehensive search that includes a critique of the studies. This leaves you with the final task of producing a synthesis of the results that should:

- Summarise the key findings
- Interpret the results, comparing and contrasting the outcomes
- Develop themes or key messages that emerge from reviewing the studies
- Conclude with recommendations and limitations of your review

Your aim, as stated at the beginning of this chapter, is to provide new insights drawn from your review of the literature: a whole that is greater than the sum of the parts.

For quantitative studies the summary may take the form of a 'meta-analysis' that combines the statistical results from many studies into one overall outcome. For example, you might find that the results from ten randomized controlled trials differ regarding whether a treatment works or not – some say it does, some say it doesn't; a meta-analysis would combine the results from the ten studies to provide an overall conclusion. This is, however, a complex statistical process and would not normally be appropriate for undergraduate students. Box 16.1 provides an illustration of this approach.

A more descriptive approach, known as 'meta-ethnography', was developed by Noblit and Hare (1988) and is used to synthesise results from qualitative studies.

Having summarised the key details from your studies (see Table 16.1) the aim is to examine the results in order to identify recurring themes/concepts, including inconsistencies across studies, and then develop your own over-arching themes. These over-arching themes will then form the basis for your own results and discussion section.

box 16.1

Systematic literature reviews can save lives

The Cochrane Collaboration produces systematic literature reviews that summarise studies of medical treatments. Their logo is shown in Figure 16.2. At first sight it looks like a meaningless abstract work of art, but what it shows are the results from seven randomised controlled trials (RCTs) that tested the effectiveness of steroids to reduce deaths in premature babies. That's the seven horizontal lines you can see (the shorter the line, the more precise the result).

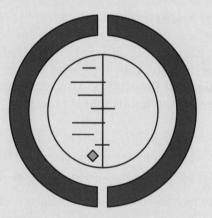

Figure 16.2 The Cochrane Collaboration logo

The vertical line is 'the line of no effect': if the horizontal lines are to the left it means the treatment works; if they are to the right it means the treatment is doing more harm than good; if they cross the vertical line, this means the trial was inconclusive. The diamond at the bottom summarises the data from the seven trials – a meta-analysis – concluding that steroids are an effective treatment to reduce deaths in premature babies. The problem was that this review wasn't conducted until many years after the individual studies, so most obstetricians didn't realise that the treatment was effective. As a result, tens of thousands of premature babies probably suffered, needed more expensive treatment than was necessary, and died (www.cochrane.org).

summary

This chapter has provided a relatively brief overview of what you need to think about when conducting literature reviews, so you may wish to look at some other more extensive sources. For example, Helen Aveyard provides a nice accessible introduction in *Doing a Literature Review in Health and Social Care* (2010), which includes a 'simplified approach' to synthesising results that may incorporate quantitative and qualitative approaches; and Trisha Greenhalgh's *How to Read a Paper* (2006) is also a classic text that discusses different types of reviews in the health sciences.

17

Presentations: a fate worse than death?

If you're dreading doing that presentation, you're not alone. A survey by OnePoll (Burgess, 2013) found that people rank fear of public speaking higher than fear of death, being buried alive, or being involved in a car crash; much lower down the list came fear of heights, snakes, fire, spiders, fat fingers, the apocalypse, and 'losing all my photographs'. The top fear was of losing family members, followed by public speaking.

Survey shows that people would rather be buried alive than give a presentation

Illustration 17.1

Unfortunately, doing presentations is just one of those experiences you'll have to endure as a student. Yes, you'll be nervous, but that's only natural. In the long term, however, it's good for you, because it gives you the chance to practice doing presentations in the relatively safe environment of the classroom: when you leave university you may have to do them for job interviews, and then as part of your job. But since you will have probably done a few presentations for your degree, you'll have gained some confidence.

The following tips are based on a survey of tutors who were asked, 'What key advice/tips would you give to students about doing presentations?' The comments addressed these six key points:

1. Keep your slides simple

2. Talk – don't read

3. Practice – know your presentation

4. Introduce and signpost

5. Be audience aware

6. Don't panic!

Tip 116: **Keep your slides clear and simple**

This was by far the most common advice from tutors. It can be tempting to cram too much information onto slides, but try to keep them simple and clear using bullet points or lists, simply worded and allowing some 'white space'. So if you find yourself making the font size smaller and smaller because you need to fit more and more on the slide, you probably need to be thinking about using two slides rather than one. Try to keep to three or four bullet points per slide. Also, it's best to use a *sans serif* font (e.g. Arial) because they don't have protruding strokes at the end of letters, so they're clearer to read (this is especially important for people with sight impairment). The clarity of your slides will be part of the marking criteria.

Comments from the survey of tutors

Slides:

- Keep your slides simple/brief, don't clutter/overcrowd with too much information – minimum information is best (try for three or four bullet points per slide)

- Don't include everything in the slides – the slide is an aid to the speaker and audience to bring the subject to life. If the audience

(Continued)

(Continued)

is reading the slide they are not focused on what you are saying, and if you are reading the slide it is not a presentation

- Images and visuals are useful to focus and anchor the attention but should not distract from the oral presentation.

- Don't bore your audience with all the details – summarize

- A presentation is a long news broadcast, not a cut-down Hollywood movie. Stick to three key messages

Version1

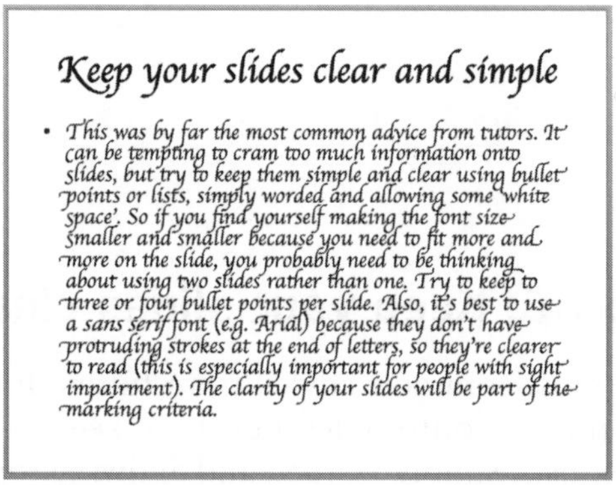

Keep your slides clear and simple

- *This was by far the most common advice from tutors. It can be tempting to cram too much information onto slides, but try to keep them simple and clear using bullet points or lists, simply worded and allowing some 'white space'. So if you find yourself making the font size smaller and smaller because you need to fit more and more on the slide, you probably need to be thinking about using two slides rather than one. Try to keep to three or four bullet points per slide. Also, it's best to use a sans serif font (e.g. Arial) because they don't have protruding strokes at the end of letters, so they're clearer to read (this is especially important for people with sight impairment). The clarity of your slides will be part of the marking criteria.*

Version 2

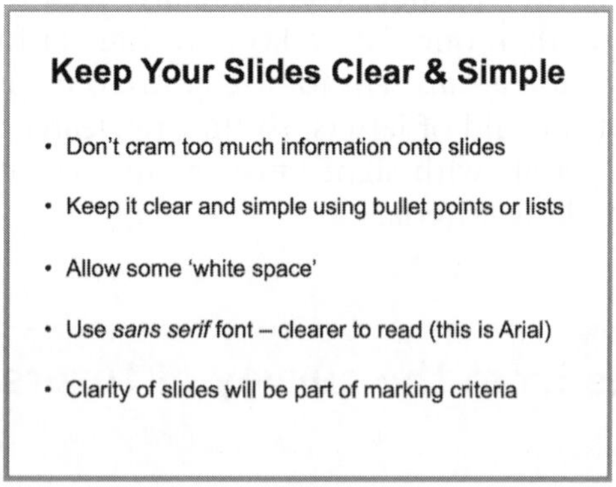

Keep Your Slides Clear & Simple

- Don't cram too much information onto slides

- Keep it clear and simple using bullet points or lists

- Allow some 'white space'

- Use *sans serif* font – clearer to read (this is Arial)

- Clarity of slides will be part of marking criteria

Figure 17.1 Keep your slides clear and simple

Take a look at Figure 17.1. It shows two versions of the paragraph above in presentation form. In the first version the information has simply been copied and pasted into the slide, but there are obviously a few things wrong here:

1. The font is a bad choice – it's too complicated; it would be better to use a sans serif font as in version 2.

2. It's simply pasted in, written as one long paragraph; version 2 simplifies the text into five bullet points.

3. Although version 2 is not particularly exciting to look at, the bullet points have made the slide clear and simple with plenty of white space.

Tip 117: Avoid annoying gimmicks

Adding some visual images can help to make the slide more attractive and interesting, but they should enhance, not distract from the information, and it's best to avoid annoying gimmicks. I remember going to a talk by a finance director in which every slide came in with a crashing sound of money. It was funny the first time, but irritating by the third slide.

Tip 118: Talk – don't read

This was the second most common comment from the tutors (it's easy for them to say, of course, they're used to it). I suspect some students like to cram their slides with lots of text because it acts as a safety net – everything is there on the screen so you can simply read it out. But you know you'll be marked down for just reading out what's on the slide. And remember, the clarity of your slides will be part of the marking criteria.

Comments from the survey of tutors

- Talk – don't read out your slides, use them to provide a structure for what you want to say (this was the most common comment)

- Reading directly from the notes will mean you are not engaging the audience

- The oral presentation is a performance. Structure the visuals and information to fit the time available and audience

- Look your audience in the eye as much as you can. Change the pitch in your voice, smile and be confident

- Use prompt cards rather than A4 paper – they shake less if you're nervous!

- Remember the presentation should enhance the information. If it doesn't, the audience could read it themselves

Tip 119: Take in a bottle of water

Because when was the last time you talked continuously for 10–15 minutes?

Tip 120: Aim to 'move comfortably within the topic'

I once heard the novelist Ian McEwan say in an interview that he needed to do lots of research for his books so he could 'move comfortably within the topic'. It's the same for all assignments, but particularly for presentations, since the slides should be there as prompts, not words to be read out loud. The more comfortable you are with the content of your slides, the easier it will be to talk around them.

Comments from the survey of tutors

- Don't read from your cue cards/notes

- Be confident with the material – know what you are going to say, but not how you are going to say it

- Know your presentation: rehearse!

Tip 121: Slow down – what's it about first?

I've been to some presentations where I was lost from the start. The first couple of slides introducing the presentation came and went in a blur without giving me chance to fully digest the topic and the aim of the presentation. Introductory overviews, as we know (Tip 23), are particularly important so that the audience has a clear idea of what your topic is about before you launch into the details. So make sure you spend some time outlining the topic and aims of your presentation.

Comments from the survey of tutors

- Use the first slide to show simply what the presentation is about

- Be sure to let the audience know what you intend to demonstrate (aims) and the types of theories and data you will be using to fulfil those aims (objective). A little roadmap at the start makes it easier for the audience to follow your presentation

- Set out your plan at the start

- Slow down, don't rush – people are interested, give them time to think

Tip 122: **The mind can only absorb what the buttocks can endure**

Numerous studies have reported that the attention of students in lectures tends to wane after 10 minutes (Wilson and Korn, 2007). Now this clearly depends on a number of factors (the speaker, the topic, etc.) but it's worth bearing in mind when giving a presentation. Keep it short and to the point.

Fortunately, most student presentations will be quite short – around 10–15 minutes – but this means you need to focus *and make sure you're within the time limit.* If you suddenly notice an alarm beeping and your tutor frantically pointing at his watch, this means you've been going on too long. At which point your talk will deteriorate into a flustered babble as you desperately rush through the remaining slides. Undignified.

So once you have a draft of your presentation make sure that you practice talking through it *out loud.* This will enable you to see how it works *as a talk,* and how long it lasts *as a talk* – compared to just running through it in your head, which is much quicker. Timing will be part of the marking criteria: not too short, but definitely not too long.

Tip 123: **The audience is on your side (usually)**

If the audience were as critical of you as you are of yourself, then you might be in trouble. But they're not (unless you're the Chancellor on Budget Day). This can be for a variety of reasons:

- politeness
- empathy with your situation
- they're not really listening
- they don't really care
- they need to be somewhere else
- or simply because *you are the expert* - having researched the topic you should know more about it than the audience

Even if they have managed to take in and remember everything you've said, there probably isn't the time to put you through the Spanish Inquisition – especially if you've overrun on purpose to avoid those awkward probing questions (though in my experience the usual response to *Any Questions?* is deathly silence followed by a ball of tumbleweed). The irony is that you'll probably find yourself going away disappointed at the lack of questions, having spent days worrying about them.

Comments from the survey of tutors

- Things often don't go quite to plan – but these things are bigger in your head than for the audience

- Don't panic if something goes wrong – just say 'excuse me' and carry on

- Try not to swear when things go wrong. It doesn't help the mark.

Tip 124: Nobody's perfect – try not to catastrophise

There's a psychological therapy that provides some comfort for people who suffer from anxiety in stressful situations. It's called cognitive behaviour therapy, and the basic idea can be summed up by the following observation from the Greek philosopher Epictetus: 'Men are disturbed not by things, but by the view they take of them.' So if you are thinking any of the following, then you may be suffering from what psychologists call 'dysfunctional thinking':

- They'll all be bored rigid

- I'm going to make an idiot of myself

- I'll probably crack up at one point

- People will laugh at me

- I'll start shaking uncontrollably

- I'll lose track and it will be a shambles

- They'll ask me awkward questions that I won't be able to answer

- I should be perfect even if this is my first presentation

- I should be funny, witty and entertaining

- I should be able to deliver this talk like Martin Luther King

I've listed a few types of dysfunctional thinking in Table 17.1 to illustrate how this might apply to doing presentations. It's never going to be as bad as you think it could be, and the important learning point is that the more presentations you do, the less panicky and more in control you will feel.

Table 17.1 Dysfunctional thinking

Type of thinking	Description	Examples
Catastrophising	Thinking the worst outcome, based upon something minor going wrong	There's a spelling mistake on the first slide - this is going to be a disaster
Mind-reading or jumping to conclusions	Assuming what others are thinking	He just whispered something to the person sat next to him - I'll bet it's a funny comment about me. She's got her eyes closed - she obviously thinks this is so boring
All or nothing	Events/things are on one extreme or another rather than the spectrum of possibilities	I should be good at presentations; I'm rubbish at everything; I'll never get anywhere
Unrealistic and high standards	Using overly high criteria for judgement of self or others. Using 'should', 'ought' and 'must'	I should be able to do great presentations. I ought to be funny and entertaining. (You're a student - not a famous motivational speaker!)

Tip 125: **Consult the marking criteria**

The specific assessment criteria will vary depending on the course and the subject matter, but there are some general criteria for the assessment of presentations. I've listed a few of these below:

Content

- Structure: Was it clearly outlined and signposted? Does it have a clear and logical structure?
- Language: Does it use clear and concise language?
- Content: Is it of sufficient depth and breadth

Presentation

- Audibility: Is it clear? Not too fast and not too slow?
- Fluency: Does it flow and show familiarity with subject?
- Tone and energy: Is there appropriate variation and emphasis (rather than a flat monotone)?
- Eye contact: Is eye contact maintained? (This will force you not just to read from your notes.)

- Clarity of slides: Are they easy to read and relevant?
- Timing: Does it fill the time allowed comfortably, without being rushed?
- Questions: Were questions invited and responded to appropriately?

Tip 126: **Don't forget the handouts**

Handouts may be specified in your assignment brief, but even if they are not, they are a welcome bonus for the audience. It is up to you when you distribute them – before or after the presentation – though if it's going to be after tell the audience so they'll know. Most people prefer to have them at the start so they can focus on the talk rather than taking notes; however, the audience may then be focused mainly on the handout and not on your well-rehearsed, Oscar-worthy performance (yeah, best hand them out at the start, then).

Tip 127: **Email it to yourself**

Finally, always email the presentation to yourself just in case anything goes wrong with your storage device. You can then retrieve it from your mailbox should the worst happen.

summary

The tips in this chapter outline what tutors are looking for when assessing presentations. The key advice is to keep your slides simple and your message clear, prepare and practice so that you can talk through your slides, and make sure it's within the time limit. As for the nerves, well, they should subside with preparation, and practice. Would you rather be buried alive? (Don't answer that.)

18

Group project work, or 'hell is other people'

It was the existentialist philosopher Jean-Paul Sartre who coined the phrase 'hell is other people' in his play *No Exit*. Three people are sent to Hell expecting to be tortured for their sins, but are surprised to find themselves simply left in a room together. As they begin to get on each other's nerves, one of the characters realises that *they* are the instruments of torture – that hell is other people! Group work can feel like this, particularly when your degree classification depends on the performance of others. I can still recall as an undergraduate witnessing a classmate scrambling over chairs and desks in a desperate bid get as much distance between himself and a particularly vociferous student who happened to be sat next to him. If group work is on the agenda, choose where you sit wisely.

On a more positive note, working with others provides the opportunity to share ideas, skills and expertise and learn from each other. Collaboration and teamwork are essential for many tasks in the real world; it would have taken one person a very long time to achieve President Kennedy's aim of 'landing a man on the moon and returning him safely to the earth'. As an old African proverb puts it: 'If you want to go fast, go alone; if you want to go further, go together.'

The key stages of project work are:

1. Define and plan
2. Assign roles and tasks
3. Monitor progress and completion of tasks
4. Review, evaluate and reflect on the project

But it is people who implement projects; so, above all, it is crucial to maintain good relationships within the group.

Tip 128: Projects fail at the start not at the end – have clear aims and objectives

The importance of a clear aim and objectives has already been discussed in Chapter 15 (Tips 108 and 109). Just to recap, the aim should be a general statement outlining the ultimate purpose of the project (e.g. the aim of this project is to produce an information leaflet for people with diabetes); and the objectives are the means used to achieve this aim. Try to make them as SMART as possible:

- **S**pecific: clearly defined with completion criteria
- **M**easureable: clear targets so you can measure progress
- **A**chievable: attainable (and agreed – so people can own them)
- **R**ealistic: given resources – time, money, equipment
- **T**ime-bound: clear timeframes

It sounds simple, doesn't it? But it isn't. Consider the project outline in Figure 18.1, where the brief is to produce a stall for a health promotion event. Are you clear from this what the aim and objectives of the project are? I wasn't. This is because the students have not spelled out a clear and simple aim. Indeed, the objectives are more like broad, vague aims; they certainly don't specify how the project will achieve them. For example, *how* will they 'educate people about obesity'? Will they be producing leaflets, doing a play, providing a video with some information about what constitutes obesity and some statistics about the associated risks? If you don't start with clear aims and objectives, your project will be like setting out on a journey without a clear destination or map.

But let's assume you have identified an aim and the relevant objectives for achieving this. What happens next? You should then be asking whether

---

Project specification

Obesity

Brief description of project

According to NHS UK obesity is the accumulation of excess fat in the body and this arises as a result of an imbalance between energy expenditure and energy intake. Obesity has a serious implication on health, such as cancer, type 2 diabetes, high blood pressure, depression, short life, mental illness. Obesity is mostly dictated by measuring body mass index (BMI). The Obese BMI is between 30 and 39.9.

Project objectives

- Educate people about obesity causes and its cost. BBC, 2012 stated that obesity cost NHS at least 500 million a year and it's growing rapidly.
- To empower people on how to eat healthy
- Motivate students on healthy lifestyle
- Keep them informed, alert, and aware of the risks associated with obesity.

Figure 18.1 A project outline with unclear aims and objectives

the aim is worthwhile. In other words, is the project worth doing? As the 'management guru' Peter Drucker (1909–2005) once remarked: 'There is nothing so useless as doing efficiently that which should not be done at all.'

Tip 129: Plan to avoid the known unknowns and the unknown unknowns

When the then US Defence Secretary Donald Rumsfeld was asked in 2002 about the lack of evidence linking the government of Iraq with the supply of weapons of mass destruction to terrorist groups, he famously replied:

> Reports that say that something hasn't happened are always interesting to me, because as we know, there are known knowns; there are things we know we know. We also know there are known unknowns; that is to say we know there are some things we do not know. But there are also unknown unknowns – the ones we don't know we don't know. And if one looks throughout the history of our country and other free countries, it is the latter category that tend to be the difficult ones.

Projects rarely go to plan, so it's important to build in time to deal with 'known unknowns' and 'unknown unknowns'.

There are various techniques to help you plan a project, but the Gantt chart is the most commonly used visual device, providing a list of the tasks that need to be completed, and by when. There is a simple example of a Gantt chart for completing an assignment in Chapter 4 (Figure 4.2), but for more complicated projects you will need to be more specific about the sub-tasks as well as identifying the people responsible for completing the tasks. For example, Figure 18.2 details the tasks involved in planning a charity event attempting to break the Guinness world record for the most people you can fit in a Mini (adapted from Maylor, 2010).

Comments from survey of tutors

- Ensure that the group has key objectives/targets to meet, clear deadlines, and particular people responsible for achieving particular tasks

- Set out ground rules and agree responsibilities and allocate tasks at the outset

- Ensure that the workload is divided fairly

- Share out the work and agree/assign clear roles

- Keep a record of meetings - who attended and what was said - and, most importantly who is going to do what

Activities	Weeks											
	1	2	3	4	5	6	7	8	9	10	11	12
Obtain car												
Contact local dealers												
Visit dealers to negotiate borrowing car												
Collect car day of event												
Arrange insurance												
Meet with university department												
Arrange insurance for driving car to site												
Continued…												

Activities	Person responsible
Obtain car	John
Contact local dealers	
Visit dealers to negotiate borrowing car	
Collect car on day of event	
Arrange insurance	Paul
Meet with university department	
Arrange insurance for driving car to site	
Organise barbeque	George
Contact university catering	
Obtain barbeque	
Ask supermarkets for free food	
Collect/purchase food day of event	
Collect BBQ day of event	
Satisfy health & safety	Ringo
Meet with health & safety	
Carry out risk assessment	
Promote event	John/Paul
Design and produce posters	
Alert local radio and newspaper	
Set up university stall on walkway	
Arrange venue	George/Ringo
Look for suitable venues	
Select venue and back-up venue	

Figure 18.2 Gantt chart and task allocation for charity event attempting to break the Guinness world record for most people you can fit in a Mini (adapted from Maylor, 2010)

Tip 130: Assigning roles and tasks: people are better at some things than others

When allocating tasks try to take into account the preferences and abilities of each member of the group. In this respect Meredith Belbin's nine team roles, summarised in Table 18.1, are a popular management tool for identifying the strengths and weaknesses of people working in teams. Which one are you?

Table 18.1 Belbin's nine team roles

Team Role	Contribution	Allowable Weaknesses
Plant	Creative, imaginative, free-thinking. Generates ideas and solves difficult problems	Ignores incidentals. Too preoccupied to communicate effectively
Resource Investigator	Outgoing, enthusiastic, communicative. Explores opportunities and develops contacts	Over-optimistic. Loses interest once initial enthusiasm has passed
Co-ordinator	Mature, confident, identifies talent. Clarifies goals. Delegates effectively	Can be seen as manipulative. Offloads own share of work
Shaper	Challenging, dynamic, thrives on pressure. Has the drive and courage to overcome obstacles	Prone to provocation. Offends people's feelings
Monitor Evaluator	Sober, strategic and discerning. Sees all options and judges accurately	Lacks drive and ability to inspire others. Can be overly critical
Teamworker	Co-operative, perceptive and diplomatic. Listens and averts friction	Indecisive in crunch situations. Avoids confrontation
Implementer	Practical, reliable, efficient. Turns ideas into actions and organizes work that needs to be done	Somewhat inflexible. Slow to respond to new possibilities
Completer Finisher	Painstaking, conscientious, anxious. Searches out errors. Polishes and perfects	Inclined to worry unduly. Reluctant to delegate
Specialist	Single-minded, self-starting, dedicated. Provides knowledge and skills in rare supply	Contributes only on a narrow front. Dwells on technicalities

Source: www.belbin.com

Belbin defines these team roles as: 'a tendency to behave, contribute and inter-relate with others in a particular way' (www.belbin.com). He found that teams with a good balance of these roles worked best:

> For example … a team with no Plants struggled to come up with the initial spark of an idea with which to push forward. However, once too many Plants were in the team, bad ideas concealed good ones and non-starters were given

too much airtime. Similarly, with no Shaper, the team ambled along without drive and direction, missing deadlines. With too many Shapers, in-fighting began and morale was lowered. (www.belbin.com)

Now obviously, you may not have the luxury of picking the members of your team according to the criteria proposed by Belbin (which requires completing an assessment), but it is important to think about who does what according to their strengths and weaknesses as group members.

Comments from the survey of tutors

- Different people have different strengths and styles with respect to group working so, where possible, work with them rather than against them

- Teamwork is the key. Make sure you consult with all members of your team regularly

Tip 131: Beware of 'social loafers'

The most common complaint about group work is directed at certain members who don't contribute and leave others to do most of the work. There is a term for these people – 'social loafers' – because they tend to put in less effort when part of a group and they can produce a great deal of resentment amongst team members.

So what should you do if certain members of the group are shirking the work? Well, after complaining first to the student and then to the tutor, you could suggest some kind of peer evaluation for the project – where each member of the group awards marks to all the other members of the group reflecting their contribution to the project, in terms of attending group meetings, contributing to discussions, and completing tasks well and on time. There are various ways to do this. If it's not already in place, ask your tutor about it.

Tip 132: Be nice – be polite

Imagine that you want someone to open a door. How are you going to ask them? Which option would you select from the following:

1. Open the door.

2. I would like you to open the door.

3. Can you open the door?

4. Would you mind opening the door?

5. May I ask you whether or not you would mind opening the door?

Personally I would probably go for option 3, but it would depend on the context. If I were asking a stranger to let me into a building because I am holding a large heavy object I might opt for 4, but if I were being chased by an angry student wielding a machete I would more likely go for 1.

The issue is one of politeness, which sometimes has to be balanced against directness: option 1 is the most direct; option 5 is the most polite. No matter how many Gantt charts and task allocation tables you produce to make sure your project is well planned, the most common issue that can scupper a project is poor relationships with other people. Successful group project work depends on fostering good relationships, so consider setting some team values at the outset – for example, to show respect and consideration; to listen to what others have to say; to contribute equally; to avoid negativity. I'm sure there are others you would like to add.

Tip 133: Keep tabs on progress: monitor and control

Try to plan your project in stages with tasks and sub-tasks, like those in Figure 18.2, so that you can monitor progress at key junctures. Keeping tabs on progress may be done by email or phone, but it is also important to schedule meetings in your plan (Gantt chart) so that you can review progress at key stages (milestones). This is a very important control mechanism for ensuring the project is still on track to achieving its objectives and ultimately fulfilling the overall aim.

Comments from the survey of tutors

- Plan your meetings, deadlines and targets in advance
- Arrange a clear schedule for the project with small achievable targets to aim for
- Illustrate tangible outputs
- Set targets for the group and individuals
- Keep evidence of plans and schedules
- Hold regular group meetings to review progress
- Check in regularly with each other and reassign tasks if key tasks haven't been completed
- Don't assume anything

Tip 134: Know how to work out the overall module mark

Feelings can run high when your mark depends on the performance of others. I recall one group of students continually bickering about the direction of their project and allocation of tasks, and when I heard one say to another 'It's no wonder you're bald, with the amount of stressing you're doing', I knew it wouldn't be long before I'd be called in to mediate.

Working out how much damage might be done by the group project to your degree classification (and hence your choice of career, and therefore your life generally) is important: you need to know how much the group project work actually accounts for the overall module mark, which often consists of an individual assignment and a group work assignment. There are various ways to allocate marks, but below I've provided a simple example.

Imagine that the group assignment is going to account for 20% of the module marks, and your own individually written assignment will account for 80%. In order to work out the mark you simply need to multiply your mark by the percentage allocated to it. Here are two illustrations.

Scenario 1. The group task is going to bring down your individual mark: you've done worse in the group task than the individual assignment:

Assignment   = 70% × 0.8 = 56%

Group Project = 50% × 0.2 = 10%

Total   = 66%

In this case, you got 70% for your individual assignment (well done) but only 50% for your group assignment (those b******s have ruined your life!). So the group task has reduced your individual assignment mark by 4%.

Scenario 2. You've done better in the group task than the individual assignment:

Assignment   = 58% × 0.8 = 46%

Group Project = 70% × 0.2 = 14%

Total   = 60%

In this case, you've improved your mark by 2% (well done for aligning yourself with a good group!).

Tip 135: Remain optimistic

Projects rarely go to plan and regularly overrun in terms of time and cost, so try to keep the following advice in mind:

- When things are going well, something will go wrong. When things cannot get any worse, they will. When things appear to be going better, you have overlooked something.

- A carelessly planned project will take three times the time expected to complete. A well-planned one will take twice as long.

Finally:

- Whatever you did, that's what you planned.

summary

The tips in this chapter outline the key ingredients for successful group projects. These require clear aims and objectives, appropriate allocation of tasks, and milestones for monitoring progress towards objectives. Most crucially though, group projects require good communication skills to promote, rather than hinder, collaboration.

References

Allport, G.W. (1969) *Pattern and Growth in Personality*. New York: Holt: Rinehart & Winston.

Arnott, D. and Dacko S. (2014) Time of submission: An indicator of procrastination and a correlate of performance on undergraduate marketing assignments. Paper presented at the European Marketing Academy. Reported at: http://www.wbs.ac.uk/news/leaving-essays-to-the-last-minute-can-ruin-your-grades/ (accessed January 2016).

Aslett, H. (2006) Reducing variability, increasing reliability: exploring the psychology of intra-and inter-rater reliability. *Investigations in University Teaching & Learning*, 4(1): 86–91.

Aveyard, H. (2010) *Doing a Literature Review in Health and Social Care*. Maidenhead: Open University Press.

Ayer, A.J. (1936) *Language, Truth and Logic*. Harmondsworth: Penguin.

Baker, M. (2015) First results from psychology's largest reproducibility test. *Nature*, 30 April. www.nature.com/news/first-results-from-psychology-s-largest-reproducibility-test-1.17433 (accessed January 2016).

Baty, P. (2006) Cheat experts in row over quote. *Times Higher Education*, 16 June.

Bausell, R. B. (2007) *Snake Oil Science: The Truth about Complementary and Alternative Medicine*. Oxford: Oxford University Press.

BBC News (2008) Cambridge students 'plagiarising'. *BBC News*, 31 October. Available at: http://news.bbc.co.uk/1/hi/education/7701798.stm (accessed January 2016).

Bhabha, H. (1994) *The Location of Culture*. Abingdon: Routledge.

Blair, A. (2005) Student work 'rife with plagiarism'. *Times Higher Educational Supplement*, 3 November.

Bloom, B. S., Engelhart, M.D., Furst, E.J., Hill, W.H. and Krathwohl, D.R. (1956) *Taxonomy of Educational Objectives: The Classification of Educational Goals, Handbook I: Cognitive Domain*. New York: David McKay.

Bloxham, S., den-Outerb, B., Hudson, J. and Price, M. (2015) Let's stop the pretence of consistent marking: exploring the multiple limitations of assessment criteria. *Assessment & Evaluation in Higher Education*. http://dx.doi.org/10.1080/02602938.2015.1024607

Brady, B. and Dutta, K. (2012) 45,000 caught cheating at Britain's universities. *Independent on Sunday*, 11 March. Available at: www.independent.co.uk/news/education/education-news/45000-caught-cheating-at-britains-universities-7555109.html (accessed January 2016)

Bransford, J.D. and Johnson, M.K. (1972) Contextual prerequisites for understanding: some investigations of comprehension and recall. *Journal of Verbal Learning and Verbal Behavior*, 11: 717–726.

Brizendine, L. (2006) *The Female Brain*. New York: Broadway Books.

Burgess, K. (2013) Speaking in public is worse than death for most. *The Times*, 20 November.

Cotrell, S. (2008) *The Study Skills Handbook* (3rd edition). Basingstoke: Palgrave Macmillan.

Coughlan, S. (2008) Overseas students 'buying essays'. *BBC News*. Available at: www.news.bbc.co.uk/1/hi/education/7275452.stm (accessed January 2016).

Covey, S.R. (2004) *7 Habits of Highly Effective People*. New York: Free Press.

Curran, J and Volpe, G. (2004) *Degrees of Freedom: An Analysis of Degree Classification Regulations*. London: London Metropolitan University.

Dann, C. (2009) From where I sit – the never-ending sentence. *Times Higher Education*, 2 July. Available at: www.timeshighereducation.co.uk/story.asp?storyCode=407183& sectionco de=26 (accessed January 2016).

Davenas, E., Beauvais, F., Arnara, J., Oberbaum, M., Robinzon, B., Miadonna, A., Tedeschi, A., Pomeranz, B., Fortner, P., Belon, P., Sainte-Laudy, J., Poitevin, B. and Benveniste, J. (1988) Human basophil degranulation triggered by very dilute antiserum against IgE. *Nature*, 333 (6176): 816–18. doi:10.1038/333816a0. PMID 2455231

Davies, J. (2013) *Cracked: Why Psychiatry is Doing More Harm Than Good*. London: Icon Books.

Defeyter, M.A. and McPartlin, P.L. (2007) Helping students understand essay marking criteria and feedback. *Psychology Teaching Review*, 13(1): 23–33.

Duggleby, W., Holtslander, L., Kylma, J., Duncan, V., Hammond, C. and Williams, A. (2010) Metasynthesis of the hope experience of family caregivers of persons with chronic illness. *Qualitative Health Research*, 20(2): 148–158.

Duncan, N. (2007) 'Feed-forward': improving students' use of tutors' comments. *Assessment & Evaluation in Higher Education*, 32(3): 271–283.

Durant, W. (1926) *The Story of Philosophy*. New York: Simon and Schuster.

Entwistle, N. (2000) Promoting deep learning through teaching and assessment: conceptual frameworks and educational contexts. Paper presented at the Teaching & Learning Research Programme Conference, Leicester. Available at: www.tlrp.org/acadpub/Entwistle2000.pdf (accessed January 2016).

Faunce, G.J. and Job, R.F.S. (2001) The accuracy of reference lists in five experimental psychology journals. *American Psychologist*, 56: 829–830.

Feldman, S. (2009) To catch a plagiarist. *Times Higher Education*, 9 July. Available at: www.timeshighereducation.co.uk/story.asp?storycode=407301 (accessed January 2016).

Fister, K. (2004) The other medicine. *British Medical Journal*, 329(7471): 923.

Foreman, M.D. and Kirchhoff, K.T. (1987) Accuracy of references in nursing journals. *Research in Nursing and Health*, 10: 177–183.

Forer, B.R. (1949) The fallacy of personal validation: a classroom demonstration of gullibility. *Journal of Abnormal Psychology*, 44: 118–121.

Fountain, T. (1999) *Resident Alien: Quentin Crisp Explains It All*. London: Nick Henn Books.

Frankfurt, H.G. (2005) *On Bullshit*. Princeton, NJ: Princeton University Press.

Garry, J., McCool, A. and O'Neill, S. (2005) Are moderators moderate? Testing the 'anchoring and adjustment' hypothesis in the context of marking politics exams. *Politics*, 25(3): 191–200.

Giles, J. (2005) Internet encyclopedias go head to head. *Nature*, 438: 900–901.

Glendinning, I. (2013) Plagiarism policies in the UK. Impact of policies for plagiarism in higher education across Europe. Available at: http://ketlib.lib.unipi.gr/xmlui/bitstream/handle/ket/790/Plagiarism%20Policies%20in%20the%20United%20Kingdom.pdf?sequence=2&isAllowed=y (accessed January 2016).

Goldacre, B. (2009) *Bad Science*. London: Harper Perennial.

Goldacre, B. (2012) *Bad Pharma*. London: Harper Collins.

Greasley, P. (2000a) Handwriting analysis and personality assessment: The creative use of analogy, symbolism and metaphor. *European Psychologist*, 5(1): 44–51.

Greasley, P. (2000b) The management of positive and negative responses in a spiritualist medium consultation. *Skeptical Inquirer*, 24(5): 45–49.

Greasley, P. (2008) *Quantitative Data Analysis Using SPSS: An Introduction for Health and Social Science*. Maidenhead: Open University Press.

Greasley, P. and Cassidy, A. (2010) When it comes round to marking assignments: how to impress and how to 'distress' lecturers…. *Assessment & Evaluation in Higher Education*, 35(2): 173–89.

Greenhalgh, T. (2006) *How to Read a Paper: The Basics of Evidence-based Medicine*. Oxford: Blackwell.

Grice, P. (1975) Logic and conversation. In P. Cole and J.L. Morgan (eds), *Syntax & Semantics 3: Speech Acts*. New York:Academic Press (pp. 41–58).

Guardian (2010) 10 rules for writers. *The Guardian*, 20 February.

Higher Education Academy (2016) *GPA Programme Outline*. Available at: www.heacad emy.ac.uk/sites/default/files/downloads/gpa_programme_outline.pdf (accessed June 2016).

Higher Education Statistics Agency (2016) *Higher Education Student Enrolments and Qualifications Obtained at Higher Education Providers in the United Kingdom 2013/14*. Available at: www.hesa.ac.uk/sfr210 (accessed May 2016).

Horton, R. (2000) Editorial. *Medical Journal of Australia*, 172: 148–149.

Huff, D. (1973) *How to Lie with Statistics*. London: Penguin.

Hussey, T. and Smith, P. (2010) *The Trouble with Higher Education: A Critical Examination of Our Universities*. Oxford Routledge.

Innovation, Universities, Science and Skills Committee (2009) *Students and Universities: Eleventh Report of Session 2008–09*, HC 170-I. London: Stationery Office.

Ioannidis, J.P.A. (2005) Why most published research findings are false. *PLoS Med* 2(8): e124.

Jaschik, S. (2007) A stand against Wikipedia. *Inside Higher Education*, 26 January. Available at: www.insidehighered.com/news/2007/01/26/wiki (accessed January 2016).

Jones, E.E., Rock, L., Shaver, K.G., Goethals, G.R. and Wand, L.M. (1968) Patterns of performance and ability attribution: an unexpected primacy effect. *Journal of Personality & Social Psychology*, 10: 317–340.

Jones, O. (2014) *The Establishment: And How They Get Away with It*. London: Allen Lane.

Jump, P. (2015) Reproducing results: how big is the problem? *Time Higher Education*, 3 September. Available at: https://www.timeshighereducation.com/features/repro ducing-results-how-big-is-the-problem (accessed January 2016).

Kangis, P. (2001) Presentational dimensions and marks awarded to assignments. *Quality in Higher Education*, 7(3): 199–206.

Keinänen, M. (2015) Taking your mind for a walk: a qualitative investigation of walking and thinking among nine Norwegian academics. *Higher Education*, http://dx.doi. org/10.1007/s10734-015-9926-2

Knipschild, P. (1994) Systematic reviews: some examples. *British Medical Journal*, 309: 719.

Kruger, J. and Dunning, D. (1999) Unskilled and unaware of it: how difficulties in recognising one's own incompetence lead to inflated self-assessments. *Journal of Personality and Social Psychology*, 77(6): 1121–1134.

Lamb, B. (1998) The spelling standards of undergraduates, 1997–98. *Journal of the Simplified Spelling Society*, J24(2): 11–17. Available at: http://spellingsociety.org/ uploaded_journals/j24-journal.pdf (accessed January 2016).

Lamb, B. (2007) Cows inseminated by seamen: errors in the English of highly selected undergraduates. Available at: http://s3-eu-west-1.amazonaws.com/plcdev/app/public/ system/files/25/original/CowsInseminatedBySeamen.pdf (accessed 13 January 2016).

Landy, D. and Sigall, H. (1974) Beauty is talent: task evaluation as a function of the performer's physical attractiveness. *Journal of Personality and Social Psychology*, 29(3): 299–304.

Larivière, V., Gingras, Y. and Archambault, É. (2009). The decline in the concentration of citations, 1900–2007. *Journal of the American Society for Information Science and Technology*, 60(4): 858–862.

Lieberman, J.K. (2005) Bad writing: some thoughts on the abuse of scholarly rhetoric. *New York Law School Law Review*, 49: 649–664.

Lilienfeld, S.O., Lynn, S.J., Ruscio, J. and Beyerstein, B.L. (2010) *50 Great Myths of Popular Psychology*. Chichester: John Wiley & Sons.

Lunsford, A.A. and Lunsford, K. (2008) 'Mistakes are a fact of life': A national comparative study. *College Composition and Communication*, 59(4).

Lyons, R.A.,Wareham, K., Lucas, M. et al. (1999) SF-36 scores vary by method of administration: implications for study design. *Journal of Public Health Medicine*, 21: 41–45.

Macedo, D. (1994) *Literacies of Power*. Boulder, CO: Westview Press.

Macrae, F. (2006) Women talk three times as much as men, says study. *Mail Online*. Available at: www.dailymail.co.uk/femail/article-419040/Women-talk-times-men-says-study.html (accessed May 2016).

Marton, F. and Säljö, R. (1976) On qualitative differences in learning, I: Outcome and process. *British Journal of Educational Psychology*, 46: 4–11.

Maslow, A.H. (1987 [1954]) *Motivation and Personality* (3rd edition). New York: Longman.

Maylor, H. (2010) *Project Management*. London: Prentice Hall.

Mehl, M.R., Vazire, S., Ramirez-Esparaza, N., Slatcher, R.B. and Pennebaker, J.W. (2007) Are women really more talkative than men? *Science*, 317: 82.

Meho, L. (2007) The rise and rise of citation analysis. *Physics World*, January. Available at: http://staff.aub.edu.lb/~lmeho/meho-physics-world.pdf (accessed January 2016)

Miles, B. (1998) *Paul McCartney: Many Years from Now*. London:Vintage.

Miller, A.G. (1970) Role of physical attractiveness in impression formation. *Psychonomic Science*, 19: 241–243.

Miller, C.M.L. and Partlett, M. (1974) *Up to the Mark: A Study of the Examination Game*. London: Society for Research into Higher Education.

Mounsey, C. (2002) *Essays and Dissertations*. Oxford: Oxford University Press.

Murakami, H. (2008) *What I Talk about When I Talk about Running*. London: Vintage.

Murdock, B.B. (1962) The serial position effect in free recall. *Journal of Experimental Psychology*, 64: 482–488.

Naylor, R. (2007) *Whose Degree Is It Anyway? Why, How and Where Universities Are Failing Our Students*. Devon: Pencil Sharp Publishing.

Neville, C. (2009a) *How to Improve Your Assignment Results*. Maidenhead: Open University Press.

Neville, C. (2009b) Student perceptions of referencing. Research paper presented at the Referencing and Writing Symposium, University of Bradford, 8 June.

Newstead, S. (2002) Examining the examiners: why are we so bad at assessing students? *Psychology Learning and Teaching*, 2(2): 70–75.

Newstead, S. and Dennis, I. (1994) Examiners examined: the reliability of exam marking in psychology. *The Psychologist*, 7: 216–219.

Newstead, S., Franklyn-Stokes, B.A. and Armstead, P. (1996) Individual differences in student cheating. *Journal of Educational Psychology*, 88: 229–241.

Newton, E. (1990) Overconfidence in the communication of intent: heard and unheard melodies. Unpublished doctoral dissertation, Stanford University, Stanford, CA.

Nickerson, R.S. (1998) Confirmation bias: a ubiquitous phenomenon in many guises. *Review of General Psychology*, 2(2): 175–220.

Nisbett, R.E. and Wilson, T. (1977) The halo effect: evidence for unconscious alternation of judgements. *Journal of Personality and Social Psychology*, 35(4): 250–256.

Noblit, G.W. and Hare, R.D. (1988) *Meta-ethnography: Synthesising qualitative studies*. London: Sage.

Norton, L. and Pitt, E. with Harrington, K., Elander, J. and Reddy, P. (2009) *Writing Essays at University: A Guide for Students by Students*. London: London Metropolitan University, Write Now Centre for Excellence in Teaching & Learning. Also available at: https://metranet.londonmet.ac.uk/fms/MRSite/psd/hr/capd/CELT-student%20facing/Writing%20Essays%20at%20University%20book.pdf (accessed January 2016).

Norton, L.S. (1990) Essay writing: what really counts? *Higher Education*, 20(4): 411–442.

Norton, L.S., Dickins, T.E. and McLaughlin Cook, N.M. (1996a) 'Rules of the game' in essay writing. *Psychology Teaching Review*, 5(1): 1–13.

Norton, L.S., Dickins, T.E. and McLaughlin Cook, N.M. (1996b) Coursework assessment: what are tutors really looking for? In G. Gibbs (ed.) *Improving Student Learning*. Oxford: Oxford Centre for Staff Development, Oxford Brookes University.

Omar, K. (2002) Poetic licence: a nation of graduates, anyone? *Daily Times*, 3 July. Available at: http://archives.dailytimes.com.pk/editorial/03-Jul-2002/poetic-licence-a-nation-of-graduates-anyone (accessed January 2016)

Owen, C., Stefaniak, J. and Corrigan, G. (2010) Marking identifiable scripts: following up student concerns. *Assessment & Evaluation in Higher Education*, 35(1): 33–40.

Park, C. (2003) In other (people's) words: plagiarism by university students – literature and lessons. *Assessment & Evaluation in Higher Education*, 28(5): 471–488.

Parkinson, N.C. (1955) Parkinson's law. *The Economist*, 19 November. Available at: www.economist.com/businessfinance/management/displaystory.cfm?story_id=14116121# (accessed January 2016).

Pauling, L. (1986) *How to Live Longer and Feel Better*. New York: WH Freeman.

Peck, J. and Coyle. M. (1999) *The Student's Guide to Writing: Grammar, Punctuation and Spelling*. Basingstoke: Palgrave Macmillian.

Perry, W.G. (1968) *Forms of Intellectual and Ethical Development in the College Years*. New York: Holt, Rinehart and Winston.

Pinker, S. (2014) *The Sense of Style: The Thinking Person's Guide to Writing in the 21st Century*. London: Allen Lane.

Quinton, S. and Smallbone, T. (2010) Feeding forward: using feedback to promote student reflection and learning – a teaching model. *Innovations in Education & Teaching International*, 47(1): 125–135.

Schumaker, J. F. (1990) *Wings of Illusion: The Origin, Nature and Future of Paranormal Belief*. Cambridge: Polity Press.

Shermer, M. (2002) *Why People Believe Weird Things*. New York: Henry Holt.

Skinner, B.F. (1964) New methods and new aims in teaching. *New Scientist*, 22 (392): 483–484.

Skok, W. (2003) A hitch-hiker's guide to learning in higher education. *BEST Practice*, 4(1): 10–12.

Smith, M. (1998) *Social Science in Question*. London: Sage.

Smith, R. (2009) Richard Smith asks who is the E O Wilson of medicine? BMJ Blogs. Available at: blogs.bmj.com/bmj/2009/03/10/richard-smith-asks-who-is-the-e-o-wilson-of-medicine/ (accessed January 2016).

Sokal, A. (1996a) Transgressing the boundaries: toward a transformative hermeneutics of quantum gravity. *Social Text*, 46/47: 217–252.

Sokal, A. (1996b) A physicist experiments with cultural studies. *Lingua Franca*, 6(4): 62–64.

Sokal, A. and Bricmont, J. (1998) *Intellectual Impostures*. London: Profile Books.

Spear, M. (1997) The influence of contrast effects upon teachers' marks. *Educational Research*, 39(2): 229–233.

Spivey, C. and Wilkes, S.E. (2004) Reference list accuracy in social work journals. *Research on Social Work Practice*, 14: 281–286.

Stothard, M. (2008) '1 in 2' admits to plagiarism. *Varsity*, 31 October.

Strack, F., Martin, L. and Stepper, S. (1988) Inhibiting and facilitating conditions of the human smile: a nonobtrusive test of the facial feedback hypothesis. *Journal of Personality and Social Psychology*, 54: 768–777.

Sussams, J. E. (1991) *How to Write Effective Reports*. Aldershot: Gower.

Taylor, G. (2009) *A Student's Writing Guide*. Cambridge: Cambridge University Press.

Taylor, L. (2009) Goodbye to all that. *Times Higher Education*, 8–14 October.

Townsend, M., Hicks, L., Thompson, J., Wilton, K., Tuck, B. and Moore, D. (1993) Effects of introductions and conclusions in assessment of student essays. *Journal of Educational Psychology*, 85(4): 670–678.

Townsend, P. (1979) *Poverty in the United Kingdom*. London: Allen Lane and Penguin Books.

Truss, L. (2007) *Eats, Shoots and Leaves*. London: Harper Collins.

Tufte, E.D. (1983) *The Visual Display of Quantitative Information*, Cheshire CT: Graphics Press.

University of Bradford (2016) Statement of academic integrity. Available from www.brad.ac.uk/legal-and-governance/breaches-appeals-complaints/breaches/statement-of-academic-integrity/ (accessed 12 January 2016).

van de Lagemaat, R. (2007) *Writing a TOK Essay*. Cambridge: Cambridge University Press.

Wainer, H. (1984) How to display data badly. *American Statistician*, 38(2): 137–147. Available at: www.rci.rutgers.edu/~roos/Courses/grstat502/wainer.pdf (accessed January 2016).

Warburton, N. (2007) *The Basics of Essay Writing*. London: Routledge.

Ware, M. and Mabe, M. (2015) The STM report: An overview of scientific and scholarly journal publishing. International Association of Scientific, Technical and Medical Publishers, The Hague. Available at: http://www.stm-assoc.org/2015_02_20_STM_Report_2015.pdf (accessed January 2016).

Wells, M. (2005) Paxman answers the questions. *The Guardian*, 31 January. Available at: http://www.theguardian.com/media/2005/jan/31/mondaymediasection.politicsand themedia.

Wiens, K. (2012) I won't hire people who use poor grammar. Here's why. *Harvard Business Review Blog Network*, 20 July. Available at: https://hbr.org/2012/07/i-wont-hire-people-who-use-poo/ (accessed 12 January 2016).

Wilson, K. and Korn, J.H. (2007). Attention during lectures: beyond ten minutes. *Teaching of Psychology*, 34(2): 85–89.

Winch, C. and Wells, P. (1995) The quality of student writing in higher education: a cause for concern? *British Journal of Educational Studies*, 43(1): 75–87.

Index